LIKE A VIRGIN

MADONNA REVEALED

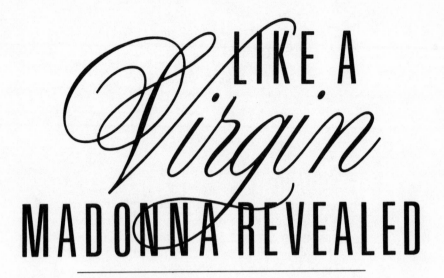

LIKE A
Virgin
MADONNA REVEALED

Douglas Thompson

SMITH GRYPHON
PUBLISHERS

First published in Great Britain in 1991 by
SMITH GRYPHON LIMITED
Swallow House, 11–21 Northdown Street
London N1 9BN

First impression October 1991
Second impression October 1991
Third impression December 1991

ISBN 1 85685 009 9

Typeset in Great Britain by Wyvern Typesetting Ltd, Bristol
Printed in Great Britain by Butler & Tanner Ltd, Frome

TO LESLEY FOR HER LOVE AND PATIENCE, AND DANDY

ACKNOWLEDGMENTS

Madonna tries to conceal herself with her version of the Official Secrets Act. All her employees must sign her control contracts swearing not to reveal *anything* about her or her lifestyle. Thankfully, secrecy pacts are made to be broken and my thanks to the many who did talk. Also to the Hollywood community from the night-club doormen to the studio chiefs – everybody has a story or opinion about Madonna.

Special thanks for help and encouragement to Katia Garritano in Rome, Ashley Williams in Hong Kong, Angela Miller in New York, Judith Chilcote in London and the diligent, digging, fact-finder Jeanne Karas in Los Angeles.

CONTENTS

Prologue

The Greatest Show on Earth

1

One

Roots

5

Two

Sexual Beginnings

17

Three

Sexual Adventures

27

Four

Cheap Popcorn

35

Five

The Deal

43

Six

The Experts

49

Seven

The Movies

59

Eight

Romantics?

71

Nine

Another Day, Another Brawl

83

Ten

Jailhouse Blues

93

Eleven

Madonnamania

101

Twelve

Bad Memories

111

Thirteen

The Top of the Hill

127

Fourteen

Breathless

139

Fifteen

The Charmer

149

Sixteen

Madonna Inc.

157

Seventeen

Leather and Lace

167

Eighteen

Hooray for Hollywood

181

Epilogue

Alone on the Hill

193

Index

195

PROLOGUE

THE GREATEST SHOW ON EARTH

'*I do think someone is protecting me. I don't know if it's an angel. It could be the Devil.*'

MADONNA IN 1990

The dazzling gown was like another of her snake skins. You expected her to slither out of it at any second. It shimmered. She shimmied. No one had ever worked the Oscars – and the ceremony's one billion television viewers world-wide – with the brassy bravado of platinum-blonde Madonna. She bumped and ground, wearing twenty-million dollars' worth of a girl's best friend. The diamonds twinkled even against the competition of her pearl-encrusted lethally low-cut dress.

The veterans ogled and said she had brought the glamour back to Hollywood and the annual cavalcade of self-acclaim – with a bang. And the roll of a hip and thrust of a buttock. If she had performed like that in the street, she would have been arrested rather than grandly and most approvingly applauded.

1

She sang the Oscar-nominated, Stephen Sondheim song 'Sooner or Later (I Always Get My Man)' from the film *Dick Tracy*. She ignited and then fanned the flames of the torch-song. The song won an Academy Award. Sizzling Madonna won the evening.

She had appeared on stage by backstage magic – an elevator lift from the orchestra pit – to gasps from the celebrity-crowded audience. Her mock strip routine was a wow especially when she turned her rear end to the crowd and simply wiggled. Even her high-profile 'date', Michael Jackson, in his gold-tipped cowboy boots, took second place to the entertainer who on Monday, 25 March 1991, at the Shrine Auditorium in downtown Los Angeles appeared on stage more like Marilyn Monroe than Monroe.

The 63rd Annual Academy Awards celebrated one hundred years of film. The traffic started jamming up around the Shrine Auditorium around 4 p.m. The Shrine holds 6200 people, which is twice as much as the Dorothy Chandler Pavilion, long-time home of the Oscars. More people but less class. There were the lines of limousines, the formally dressed men and the carefully coiffured and gowned women. But they were serving hot dogs and snacks and wine in paper cups on what is supposedly Hollywood's champagne and caviar night. This was tacky in Tinseltown.

By 6 p.m. at the Shrine the atmosphere was decidedly down at heel. The excitement level measured a zero on the Richter earthquake scale. Then, came a seismic roar from the crowds in the bleachers. Madonna had arrived. With Michael Jackson.

The tinsel was back in town. Madonna waltzed her way into the Awards as though she owned them. The pearls on her white gown played laser games with popping flashbulbs. Photo opportunity? No, this was paparazzi heaven.

Inside, Madonna and Jackson, also in white and bejewelled, took the two front-row aisle seats, centre stage. Throughout the auditorium people craned their necks to get a better look. Dustin Hoffman stood up to see what was going on. *Dick Tracy* co-star, Al Pacino, waved. *Everyone* wanted Madonna's attention. Later, during a commercial break and away from the television cameras, master of ceremonies, Billy Crystal, peered down from the stage at Madonna and enquired: 'Who do you have to fax to get on the show?' Ironically, it was the evening that Kevin Costner and his *Dances With Wolves* rode off with seven Oscars. The good guys won.

But so did the Bad Girl. The entertainment-world's commercial chameleon had just performed to her biggest audience ever. And it was a captive audience. Satellites in the sky had beamed her backside to the world's television audience. She had shook it at them. A super-confident superstar?

Probably only from the front-row seats at the Shrine, where you could see close-up and 'live', could you also see the shakes. Watching from there you could see that she was as nervous as anyone might be performing on such an evening. Madonna nervous? Oh, yes. For despite her backside-to-the-world image, this is a still insecure multi-millionairess. She still does not have all that she wants. Every bump and grind on Oscar night had been rehearsed again and again and again by this perfectionist performer.

She is determined to be the best. To be the boss. To be in total control. Madonna Louise Veronica Ciccone is determined. Period. It is in her genes.

ONE

ROOTS

'Io sono fiera di essere italiana'

('I'm proud to be an Italian')

MADONNA TO 65,000 ITALIAN FANS AT FLORENCE'S FOOTBALL STADIUM IN 1987

━━━━━━━

Gaetano Ciccone was nineteen. His new bride, Michelina, was a year younger. They were living with his family in the easy-going community of Pacentro at the foot of Mount Amaro in central Italy. It was 1919, the First World War was over and the world was changing. In Pacentro, it was for the worse. The people were farmers. They were also poor. But it was a pleasant place to live. Families left their doors unlocked. There was no crime. There was also no work or the prospect of it in Milan in the north or in Rome to the west.

A short, wiry and determined man, Gaetano Ciccone had to make a decision for himself, his bride and the babies they talked about having. He wanted lots of sons. She wanted daughters. They both wanted a good life. They had to emigrate or starve. For

Gaetano Ciccone, who is recalled in Pacentro as a feisty, driven character, there was no choice.

America, the New World, was a magnet for the poor of Europe. It offered so much. Those who had gone and returned did so in style. Between 1920 and 1930 there were 455,315 Italian immigrants to the United States and that was despite the Immigration Act of 1924 which assigned Italians an annual quota of only 3845 immigrants. In 1920, Gaetano and Michelina Ciccone were two of them. They arrived in America with Prohibition and a couple of battered suitcases. They could speak no English.

They had made the trek from Pacentro to Sulmona and then the 186 miles from there to Naples by road. It was a dusty and hungry trip, but they were young and strong. Emotionally, it was more torturous. They were leaving the stability of their home and families and investing their hopes, their very lives, in an alien culture and country. It was a gamble, a chance to profit by risk.

The voyage from Naples on the SS *Regina d'Italia* of the Lloyd Sabaudo line had taken eleven weeks. They were in steerage which meant sleeping on deck in chaffing salt-water damp blankets. On 29 April 1920, the *Regina d'Italia* entered Upper New York Bay and sailed on past the Statue of Liberty and the final three-quarters of a mile towards Ellis Island. Gaetano and Michelina Ciccone were up close to the rails along with all the other passengers. Their eyes dazzled as they stared out at their new unknown land and future.

The *Regina d'Italia* anchored at quarantine. Inspectors and immigration officials boarded to survey the latest delivery from crowded Europe. The passengers were many, the formalities swift. Along with the others, the Ciccones were put on barges and ferried to Ellis Island. All those who have walked down the gang-plank and up the quay to the New World recall the noise of the ground-floor baggage room. It was in every way a Babel. And above the smell of the masses there was the welcome aroma of thick soups, stews and freshly baked bread. Medical and legal examinations took place in the Great Hall upstairs. The Ciccones waited on wooden benches for their turn, a manifest tag with two numbers attached to their worn coats. They were each asked thirty questions in two minutes. In English. 'What is your name?' 'Where were you born?' An interpreter stood by as the Ciccones were quizzed in parrot fashion. 'Are you an anarchist?' 'Do you have a criminal record?' 'Do you have any skills?'

Gaetano Ciccone had no skills. He had strengths. He was able-bodied. He wanted 'honest work' to support his family. This was still a time of the *padrone* at Ellis Island. These were labour bosses who spoke Italian and English, who understood the ways of the Old World and the needs of the New World. They had contacts with industrial concerns throughout New York, New Jersey, Pennsylvania and southern New England.

By then, mutual-benefit societies had replaced the extended families of the Italian villages like Pacentro which today is home to only 1496 people. In 1920, 'Sons of Italy' had 125,000 members in 887 lodges across America. They helped with sickness, despair and death; it was a system to provide inexpensive group insurance.

When on 1 May 1920 the Ciccones officially stepped on to American soil, the law that was to lead to turbulent times, to the Roarin' Twenties, had been passed. The 18th Amendment and the Prohibition Enforcement (Volstead) Act of 26 January 1920 launched great groups of Italian Americans as crime entrepreneurs. At the same time the rise of Mussolini and fascism in Italy forced many Mafia leaders to make a similar, if more comfortable, trip as the Ciccones. English was bastardized: *visci* (whiskey) was what the *ghengas* (gangs) were selling on the *strittos* (streets).

The immigrants loved the music halls which were free (the profits came from liquor sales) and the opera. Cleofante Campanini was the first conductor and director of the Metropolitan Opera House. Giulio Gatti Casazza was general manager from 1908 to 1934. The Italian cultural overhaul of the New World was well in progress. So was the popular one – Frank Sinatra, Dean Martin and Tony Bennett would go on to become musical legends.

And Gaetano Ciccone looked around in bewilderment. But he heard the words 'hard work' and 'best pay'. And he understood them. He and his wife went to Pittsburgh, an inland port and one of the world's greatest steel centres and headquarters to some of America's biggest corporations. There were ferries to transport the newcomers one mile to Manhattan or only 300 yards to the piers of New Jersey where most immigrants settled. But, again, Gaetano Ciccone decided on the longer journey and the greater risk in hope of greater profit.

The days started early and finished late. The Ciccones worked hard. They moved into a rented one-bedroom house near the steel mill in a very poor, but proud, Little Italy ghetto. They did not need to learn English – everyone spoke Italian. Gaetano Ciccone got his dearest wish – sons. Six of them. And he raised them Old World style. As the father, he was the interpreter of all their needs and interests. His authority was total and he maintained it by strict discipline. It was the same for all the families. Children were given responsibility at an early age. Daughters did not work: they prepared for marriage at home and were expected to marry the spouses chosen by their parents. But things were changing in the New World. In 1919 a study in New York showed that ninety-one per cent of girls of more than fourteen years old were working for wages – and in turn, of course, an independence unknown in the Old Country.

But in Pittsburgh, Gaetano Ciccone ruled the house old-time style. The aim was to keep the family unit together. Five of his sons went into the steel mills. Silvio 'Tony' Ciccone was the youngest and most doted upon. The 'baby' of the family, he went to college and got a degree in engineering. There were no openings for optic and defence engineers in a steel town. Short and wiry and in other ways like his father, he left the stability of home and moved to where the work was.

Silvio Ciccone wanted to better himself. He was of the New World but he was also his father's son. Discipline, honesty and hard work were the creed. Integrity was the byword: teach by example. The Catholic Church provided a helpful rule book as a guide. He had never wanted for a necessity, but as the youngest of a poor immigrant family, he had had a hand-me-down upbringing. It is easy to understand the deep need to provide and provide well. And that meant having the confidence not to follow the herd. Clever and inventive, he put in the hours at several car companies in the Detroit area, in the city that would ironically become famous for the Motown – Motor Town – sound. And, later, for his daughter, an anything but assembly-line product.

When he was called up for the Armed Services, he was skilled enough to join the United States Air Force – you had to join the Air Force: they put you in the Army or Navy. He was a straight-shooter and well liked. Another airman, Michael Fortin, came from Michigan and they travelled back from a Georgia posting together. Fortin introduced Silvio Ciccone to his youngest sister – a stunning looking woman called Madonna. They fell hopelessly in-love-at-first-sight. A French-Canadian, Madonna Fortin was born in Bay City, a chill of a place on Lake Huron's Saginaw Bay. And that is where Silvio Ciccone went to visit with his future bride's family.

By then he had left the Chrysler Corporation and was working for General Dynamics. There was a post-war boom – the motor industry sold 9.3 million cars in 1955 and suburban housing tracts were changing the lifestyle aspirations of the working and middle classes. It was the days of the American Dream of Happy Families – the stereotype was television's *Father Knows Best* with Robert Young – a colour television and a garage with two cars. Marriage seemed a perfectly wonderful idea. The full-scale white wedding took place in a church in Rochester, which was then a new and developing community, not the urban sprawl it is today. Then, as now, much of the cities were lumped together as 'Detroit'.

In 1957, with Eisenhower in the White House, their first son Anthony was born. A year later Martin arrived. The following summer another child was due. The family wanted to escape the overbearing heat that comes up and off the Great Lakes in July and August. Silvio Ciccone took the family north to stay with his in-laws in Bay City.

The legend-to-be was born on 16 August 1959, a hot, sunny day when the only clouds in the sky were man-made ones from the factories and chemical dumps. It was a remarkably easy birth. The Ciccone's first daughter seemed anxious to get on with her life.

The world was changing. Castro had taken control in Cuba. John F. Kennedy was on his way to the White House. Without 'Evita', Juan Peron had been overthrown in Argentina. Antonioni's then avant-garde *L'Avventura* was being filmed. Jack Kerouac had published *On the Road*. Americans were being told they did not have to conform and that same message was circling the rest of the world.

And another non-conformist had joined it.

The day Madonna Louise Veronica Ciccone was born, Elvis Presley was atop the American pop charts with 'A Big Hunk O' Love' having knocked Paul Anka with 'Lonely Boy' from the number-one spot. It was an important week for Elvis who was serving with the United States Army in Germany – he was introduced to fourteen-year-old Priscilla Beaulieu, the daughter of an army captain, who would become his wife and part of the Elvis legend.

This was the news the Ciccones heard on the radio and read in the *Rochester Eccentric*, the local newspaper, while baby Madonna rolled around in diapers. How could they have imagined in not so many years their bald baby daughter's name would be as well known around the world as The King's?

Madonna was obviously named after her mother – but it was not an obvious thing to do. It marked her as something special from the start: it was rare for an Italian-Catholic mother to pass on her name, especially such an exotic one with all of its religious implications.

The annual birth pattern continued. Her sister Paula was born in 1960, then Christopher and Melanie. Six kids. One salary. Tough, but for Silvio Ciccone possible.

I think my earliest memories go back to about four or five years old and they're memories of my beautiful mother. They're really great memories. When I was four and younger, I remember not being able to sleep at night. I would walk to my parent's bedroom and push the door open. They were both asleep in bed and I think I must have done this a lot, gone in there, because they both sort of sat up in bed and said: 'Oh no, not again.' and I said: 'Can I get into bed with you?'

I always went to sleep right away when I slept with them. I felt really lonely and forlorn even though my brothers and sisters were in my room with me. I wanted to sleep with my parents.

I remember, because my mother had a really beautiful red nightgown, silky red. My father was against me getting into bed with them and I remember getting into bed and rubbing against her nightgown and going to sleep – just like that.

To me that was Heaven, to sleep between my parents.

What happened next was to tear her young life apart and brand and mould her future. Nearly thirty years later she is still dealing with it and regularly seeing a woman psychiatrist in Beverly Hills.

Her mother died of breast cancer at the age of thirty. A couple of years later her father remarried. She felt abandoned by one and betrayed by the other. A lost little girl. It is in her work, in her videos and songs. She will live with it forever. One friend, Lori Jahns, told me that even when they were out on wild dates her 'best friend' Madonna – she called her 'Mud' and they wrote affectionate letters to each other for several years – would often grow quiet and say: 'I miss my mother.'

Years later, Madonna keeps a photograph of her mother in a silver frame on an antique bedside table in the bedroom of her art-filled home at the top of the Hollywood Hills. The art is worth millions but the snapshot of a sixteen-year-old dark-haired girl in a long, white dress is priceless, and a constant reminder of her mother's early death. Another favourite is of herself, aged seven, wearing her mother's wedding gown and veil.

The death goes on hurting. Painfully. It is always in her words:
When I see my girlfriends with their mothers even now I can't even imagine
– it's unfathomable what that sort of nurturing would have done for me. I
really miss it. My role models who nurtured me when I was growing up were
all men. It's true. Life is just too short and I have too many goddam things
to do, so I better hurry up. That has a lot to do with my mother's death –
I've felt that way since I was a child. I think the biggest reason I was able to
express my self and not be intimidated was by not having a mother. Women
are traditionally raised to be subservient, passive, accepting. The man is
supposed to be the pioneer. He makes the money, he makes the rules. I know
that some of my lack of inhibition comes from my mother's death. For
example, mothers teach you manners. And I absolutely did not learn any of
those rules and regulations.

She watched her mother waste away from breast cancer. It
took a year, an agonizing one of futile treatments, pain-killers and
then the morphine-induced hazy, hanging-on days until the end.
Of any subject – and she has proved she is not afraid of any – this
is the one where she finds most eloquence for her emotions:
I remember her being a very forgiving, angelic person. I have a memory of
my mother in the kitchen scrubbing the floor. She did all the housekeeping
and she was always picking up after us. We were really messy, awful kids. I
remember having these mixed feelings. I have a lot of feelings of love and
warmth for her, but sometimes I think I tortured her. I think little kids do
that to people who are really good to them. They can't believe they are not
getting yelled at or something so they taunt you. I really taunted my mother.
I remember, I also knew she was sick for a long time with breast cancer so
she was very weak but she would continue to go on and do things she had to
do. I knew she was very fragile and getting more fragile.

I knew that because she would stop during the day and just sit down on
the couch. I wanted her to get up and play with me and do the things she did
before. I know she tried to keep her feelings inside and not let us know. She
never complained. I remember she was really sick and was sitting on the
couch. I went up to her and I remember climbing on her back and saying,
'Play with me, play with me' and she wouldn't. She couldn't and she started
crying and I got really angry with her, pounding her back and saying, 'Why
are you doing this.' Then I realised she was crying.

I remember feeling stronger than she was. I was so little and I put my arms around her and I could feel her body underneath me sobbing and I felt like she was the child. I stopped tormenting her after that.

She spent about a year in the hospital and I saw my father going through changes. He was devastated. It was awful to see your father cry. But he was very strong about it. He would take us to the hospital to see her and I remember my mother was always cracking up and making jokes. She was really funny so it wasn't so awful going to visit her there.

Then my mother died. I remember that right before she died she asked for a hamburger. She wanted to eat a hamburger because she couldn't eat anything for so long and I thought that was very funny. I didn't actually watch her die.

Then everything changed.

And so, she says, had she, 'That was the turning-point. The die was cast. I think that made me grow up fast. I knew I could be either sad or take control and say it's going to get better.'

After his wife's death, Silvio Ciccone was forced to separate his family. It was crushing – the patriarch was meant to keep his family together. But how could he work and care for his children? The solution, some months later, came from hiring housekeepers. This brought the children back together. One housekeeper. Then another and another. The children's behaviour was wild – a throwback to their easy-going mother.

I think my parents pissed a lot of people off because they had so many kids and they never screamed at us. My older brothers were rambunctious and they would start fires in the basement or throw rocks at windows and my mother and father would never yell at them. They would just hug us and wrap their arms around us and talk to us quietly.

It was a cosy time before death intruded. She recalls her father's 'intregrity' – she did not agree with all his Old World values or, come to that, some of the New World ones – and his living by example.

A lot of parents tell their kids not to smoke cigarettes and they smoke cigarettes. Or they give you some idea of sexual modesty – but my father lived that way. He believed that making love to someone is a very sacred thing and it shouldn't happen until after you are married. He stuck by those beliefs and that represented a very strong person to me. He was my role model. I was my father's favourite. I knew how to wrap him around my finger. I knew there was no other way to go besides saying, 'No, I'm not going to do it.' I employed those techniques. I was a very good student. I got all As. My father rewarded us for good grades. He gave us quarters and fifty cents for every A we got. I was really competitive and my brothers and sisters hated me for it. I made the most money of every report card. I'd pit myself against all of them. It wasn't because I was going to learn; it was because I wanted to be the best. Of course, all my brothers and sisters wanted to beat me up.

She could handle that. But the piano! Her father made all the children learn a musical instrument and take a daily lesson. She did piano. She hated it. She convinced her father with those young wiles to allow her to take dance lessons, tap and jazz and baton twirling. She says the classes were hangouts for hyperactive girls with no other productive means of expressing their energy.

And she had to cope with equally rowdy brothers who would hang her up on the clothes-line by her knickers. She says she always talked out of turn and her sister Paula, a tomboy, and the boys would gang up on her. She ratted on them to her father. He was Daddy Dearest. But he also brought the news that wrecked her world and still shakes it today. The tension among those trying to get on with living was at times intolerable.

'My father told me my mother was dead but you keep waiting for her to come back. We never all sat down and talked about it. I guess we should have.' Her mother's death turned her into a pre-teen anxiety case totally overdependent on her father. She would be physically sick when he left the house for longer than it took to put out the garbage. She was frightened he too would leave. She thought she had cancer. She would creep into her father's bed every night. 'I kept telling him that if he ever died, I was going to be buried in the casket with him. He would say, "Don't talk like that – that's really disgusting."' What she found utterly disgusting was his decision to marry again.

And after her father's decision to remarry, she took some peculiar revenge. Even she does not know where her mind was then, but she decided she would never again visit her mother's grave. For now, she wanted to be Cinderella. She revoked on this warped decision – but only in 1990.

TWO

SEXUAL BEGINNINGS

'*Pappa Don't Preach*'

THE SECOND SINGLE FROM MADONNA'S 1986 ALBUM, *TRUE BLUE*

Madonna and her brothers and sisters never took to their housekeepers. Who could replace their mother who died tragically early at the age of thirty? Madonna felt she too would die young. There was loneliness, a longing just for something; later she would call it 'an emptiness – if I hadn't had that, I would never have been so driven.' There was also fear. There were stairs in her house with spaces between the steps. She thought the Devil was in the basement and would always dash up the stairs so he would not grab her by the ankles. Illogical, yes, but although she was scared, she still scooted up these stairs.

She was not so quick to react to the demands of the house-keepers who seemed to spin through the home as though they were on a roundabout. Women small and tall, big and trim, young, middle-aged but all strangers. It was hard to accept discipline from strangers: wash the dishes, tidy the room, make the bed and on and on in a domestic litany. But there was one, Angelica Roberts, who resembled the late Natalie Wood. The kids liked her. Their father, however, married another housekeeper, Joan Stone. Madonna had to compete with another woman for her father's attention. And then there were more babies. Her step-sister Jennifer in 1968 and, on the annual cycle, Mario the following year.

They all lived in a two-storey colonial home just off Old Perch Road in Rochester, in a little court of homes called Oklahoma. Madonna was the oldest girl. She took care of business – and that was changing the babies' diapers. It was a torturing time but also character building and either good or bad depending on your viewpoint. Her father insisted on church before school every day. After school, the uniform came off and there were jobs around the house. There was homework, dinner and no television except for the Saturday morning cartoons. The rest of television was sinful. The family never went out to the cinema or out to dinner. Magazines were a luxury. It was like the winding of a spring as though in readiness for the drive and energy she would need to achieve so much fame and fortune in less than a decade. It was also the birth of the Madonna style – or lack of it.

Her father insisted they called his new wife 'mother' or 'mom'. But to Madonna she was her 'stepmother' and she could do no right. Madonna was not allowed tampons because her mother said they were the equivalent of sexual intercourse. To stop arguments, all the girls were bought similar dresses. Madonna hated to look like her sisters, detested the uniform required by her Catholic schools. She put bows in her hair and would wear razzle-dazzle socks. Her inside joke was her brightly coloured underpants which she wore instead of the regulation dark-blue knickers. It did not stay a secret for long – the children would tease each other by lifting up their skirts: most girls were mortified. Madonna retaliated with an unexpected flash of pink pants or black-and-white polka dots. If no one lifted her skirt, teachers recall her regularly taking solo action during school breaks and hanging upside down on the playground monkey bars revealing her rainbow of underwear.

She desperately wanted to be the oddball. Her brother Martin, now a gleaming, curly-haired good-looking disc jockey with a Detroit radio station recalls: 'She wasn't rich, she wasn't famous then, but she was the same girl – always being different from the others.' She was closest to her brother Christopher who is now an interior designer in Los Angeles: 'In an Italian home, socializing always centred around the kitchen so Madonna and I both know the value of a good pot to make a big batch of pasta.' They remember Madonna always seeking attention: climbing on to tables and dancing at family get-togethers.

By the age of ten – fifth grade in the American school system – Madonna had turned into a precocious little flirt. She was socializing outside the family circle and by now adept at getting herself noticed. She had long dark hair, a winning smile and sweet look. It was a glossy veneer and the start of the incredible play acting that would finally result in the self-sustaining phenomenon of Madonna, the Act.

The family attended St Andrews Church in Rochester and Madonna went to the Holy Family Regional School which is a rather forboding looking building on the outskirts of town. Today, things are not so strict but headmistress Mrs Sylvia Trepanier laughed: 'I'm not sure we would want to acknowledge Madonna as a former pupil.'

And that was as much reference to the past as the present. Ten-year-old Madonna was a terror. Ask Tommy, the child with bad teeth whom she chased around the playground. Madonna really went after her young man. She tore off her school blazer and white blouse and went topless after him. One of the nuns grabbed her and furiously explained that little girls did not take off their clothes and chase boys.

Until that moment she had been obsessed with becoming a nun. She thought they were so special, very beautiful: 'I saw them as really pure, disciplined, sort of above-average people. They never wore any make-up and they had these really serene faces. Nuns are sexy.' Of course, they did not chase boys. Her career goals were nun or movie star. Looking back she says just nine months of convent school put her well off the first idea. But not off Tommy – 'I wanted him'. The day after the playground chase, she received her first kiss. From Tommy. In the convent. Today, she still recalls the moment as 'incredible'. Madonna's first kiss in a convent. Well, what else?

It was the start of the rebellion. And her sexual revolution:
Probably about the same time as I began to rebel against the church I went through puberty. That was when I really started to think about sex, about its presence, not about what I was going to do about it.

Carol Belanger, a friend who was in the Brownies with her, recalls the convent days, the interest in sex – and what the nuns had beneath their habits: 'Madonna and I went peeking through the windows of the convent to see the nuns without their habits. We found out they had hair.' Belanger, who is married and still lives in the Rochester area, often attended church with Madonna. Once they went naked – under their coats. As they sat through the services, they exchanged knowing glances and supressed giggles.

Schoolfriends remember Madonna as the girl who was willing to take all the risks. If there were apples to steal, she would lead the group. When they went on shoplifting sprees, she would regularly get away with the most loot. She wore pants to church, which her father hated.

Her first great public dare was at St Andrew's annual talent show. She was in the seventh grade, but a fast-developing twelve-year-old. The parishioners gathered early in the church hall. Fathers had come home early from the car factories, showered and put on collars and ties. Mothers were wearing their Sunday dresses. And most of the kids were in their Sunday best, reciting poetry or tap dancing or singing or playing the piano.

Madonna came on stage nude. Well, she looked naked. It was her turn as Goldie Hawn from the *Laugh In* show of the sixties when Hawn used to gyrate her body, adorned with a skimpy bikini and paint. Silvio Ciccone's little girl wore green-fluorescent paint and what could be mistaken for a monokini. The music started – blasting 'Baba O'Reilly' by The Who. Under a black light which reflects fluorescent colours and 'kills' other images, Madonna wiggled and undulated and leaped about on stage with a strobe flashing. The only thing not moving were the parents' eyeballs. They were frozen in shock. The kids, especially the boys, were turned on by Madonna's first public performance. She had spent weeks planning her act, the costumes, the antics. Her father took thirty seconds to grab her as she left the stage. She was 'grounded' for two weeks. She can smile about it now: 'He was mortified. He just about dismembered me.'

As she went into her teens, Madonna became wilder rather than tamer. And also curious. About her body, about boys. About everything.

There were also the other kids at school:

You want to identify with somebody as you are growing away from being a child. You're starting to think differently and you want to be independent, but before you reach that independence you want to attach yourself to someone. In school there were hippies – the more *free* group, the guys with long hair who took a lot of jewellery and shop [trade] classes and smoked a lot of pot during lunch hour. I didn't identify with them because I thought they were extremely lazy. Then there was a jock group and they were drunk on beer everyday. I was a cheerleader for a little while, but I couldn't get into it. It wasn't that I didn't like athletics – I couldn't get into the sensibilities of cheerleaders and athletes. They were only interested in sports, drink and girls. I had this idea that everyone went to junior high and high school with blinders on their eyes and it really pissed me off. I was sure everyone was missing something and I wandered around aimlessly. My best friends were the guys who were really studious like physics majors.

But it was not easy being anybody's friend. The boys wrongly thought she was easy. The girls thought she was too. An attractive blonde called Katrina made her suspicions known after her boyfriend started flirting with Madonna. She slapped Madonna's face. On the street. In front of much of the school. Madonna was devastated. But not enough to slow down. She was listening to Diana Ross and the Supremes and young Stevie Wonder. Frankie

Lymon's songs made her weak at the knees. And she would let everyone know what she thought. 'Sometimes I literally put my hand over her mouth to shut her up,' says Carol Belanger.

A group of bikers once dropped firecrackers on us. Madonna yelled at them and told them to knock it off. One of the biker girls came down and started hitting her in the mouth. We finally got away, but she had a black eye and a bruised cheek.

At home, Silvio Ciccone still ran a strict ship. Madonna had to go to a friend's house to see television shows like *Dark Shadows* (the cult black-and-white vampire series which in 1991 was revived on United States' television with British actor, Ben Cross, as the lead vampire) and drool over David Cassidy in *The Partridge Family*. *The Monkees* was another favourite show.

She had fights with her father and they were mostly about religion. She would find ways to say she was going to a different Mass than him and then take off with her friends. But she always thought ahead and worked out the 'sermon' she had heard, to stop being caught out by her father if he quizzed her.

The Rochester school system had a more solid reputation than Madonna did on the school playground. Silvio Ciccone decided to take his oldest daughter out of Catholic school and she joined Rochester West Junior High.

She wanted to be 'European'. She stopped shaving her legs and her armpits. She wore gypsy-style clothes, and she became friends with Lori Jahns, who is now an attractive woman, married and living an hour's drive from Rochester in a smart suburban area near Hummer Lake. 'Mud' Ciccone and Lori Jahns developed together. Lori, a quick, smart, blonde sipped her Miller Lite beer and fondly recalled her Madonna days.

We were real close in eighth grade. She had other friends, but it was *us*. We sent letters back and forth and we'd call each other all the time – spend the night together if we could. I guess, back then, you always had a best friend. We had friendship rings and all that kind of jazz. She'd had a tough time at the Catholic school. Too strict. I guess the nuns were real bitches. They were just so strict and nasty and she would tell jokes about stuff she and the other kids would try and get away with.

That's why she was going nuts when she got to public school. For someone who had had to wear a uniform to school to just go to your closet and say 'I wanna wear this!' was wonderful. Or to go to a friend's house and go: 'Oh, I have twice the wardrobe now.' Hot pants were big back then and those God-awful bell-bottom jeans, those hip-huggers. She loved to borrow clothes and stuff. If it's your best friend, then it's fine. The clothes she had weren't that great. I guess it wasn't as big a deal to her family as it was to some others.

My mom didn't like her very much. She thought she'd lead me astray. She thought there was something different about her. She would never say why. Maybe it was because of her independence or because she was very headstrong. Her family was different from my family. My family always seemed to be close and dinner time was when you sat down and chatted. And it didn't seem that close at her house.

We were into boys, boys and more boys. Girls mature quicker than guys and she wrote to me about two boys saying she wished they'd grow because they were so adorable. They were short and really cute but was like, 'Hmm, this doesn't look right.'

We did a lot of boy talk and girl stuff. We'd sit around and sing. She would sing. Carole King was real big then and we'd sing her songs. And there was just all kinds of guys who would get together and practise music in someone's garage or basement. That was a big thing so they could play at high-school dances. She knew a guy down the street and we went there dancing. They said: 'Let's just goof around, why don't you guys sing back-up?' I don't even know what song it was. It was 'Proud Mary' or something like that. I didn't sing. I danced. And she got up and sang back-up. She wasn't frightened at all.

She was fearful at times. She didn't get along well with her stepmother.

Lori recalls it as a hard time for Madonna's family.

Her father was doing two jobs. There was a new woman in their home getting dad's attention. She was her mother's baby because she was the first girl. It was very seldom that she would talk about it, and when she did, she was very emotional about it. Seeing her mom die had such an impact on her. She mentioned her mom's suffering and when she did talk about it she would always say, 'I wish my mom were here.' It was always sad. I couldn't pinpoint anything that started conversations like that. She must think about her mom all the time. I'm sure she does even now.

About being a loner?

She said it gave her commitment, she wanted to do something. She'd say, 'Fine, I'm gonna do this. I *can* do this.' I think that has a lot to do with her today. It was like her dancing. We did a talent show in the eighth grade and she wanted me to do this dance number with her. She choreographed it herself and everything and I still remember the song and the lyrics, 'Let our body feel the music and feel the beat and just kind of groove to the music.' I mean, she would just dance like you could not believe. She was loose. She could really do it.

Lori says:

Madonna didn't care what anybody thought. She was just being her own self. 'I wanna do what I wanna do' was her motto. And that's what she eventually did.

Her father was one stickler for homework. You did your homework before you did anything else. She was very intelligent. I would have to study, study, study to get my Bs and As. I had to work a lot harder than she did to get the same results.

She shared a bedroom with her sisters Paula and Melissa then. A lot of times I'd ask her to come over to my house and she couldn't because she had to watch the little kids because her stepmom was doing something. Her father wasn't around a lot. He worked a lot of hours. It was a hard time for her. It was a development time. And she was a *lot* more developed than some of us. But she wasn't easy or a sleaze as we'd call it back then. I've read things that say she's had her boobs done and this and that. She never did. She always had a gorgeous figure.

Bi-sexual?

It raises a little controversy and gets people talking. But back at school, it was just boys as far as I know. But kids experiment.

The friends began going to catechism together.

I wasn't a Catholic. My mother asked: 'Why do you want to go to catechism?' 'It's interesting, Ma. You learn about different things.' I learned about boys and so did Madonna.

That's when you're finding out your sexuality and everything else. We'd do a lot of heavy petting. In a sense there was peer pressure to be cool. But at the same time, we wanted to be our own individuals. And that's hard at that age when you're trying to find out what and who you are.

Rochester was a very small, beautiful town then. You wouldn't know it anymore. It's overdeveloped, the roads can't handle the traffic. When we all first lived there, there was the golf course and the cow pasture and we could ride our bikes and go to Baskin-Robbins for ice cream.

Or we would skip catechism and go to the movies. Of course, we sat there and kissed with the boys in the front row of the movie theatre. Necking with the guys from catechism.

It was then that Madonna invented her 'floozy' look. The girls knew their parents didn't like it and that made it even more fun.

Madonna herself has a few words to add.

We got dressed to the nines. We got bras and stuffed them so our breasts were overlarge and wore really tight sweaters – we were sweater-girl floozies. We wore tons of lipstick and really badly applied make-up and huge beauty marks and did our hair like Tammy Wynette. We posed. We took turns lounging on the bed with our hands behind our head. We took pictures of each other and developed them and these were our ten-cent-floozy pictures.

Madonna the floozy moved to Rochester-Adams High School and her friend Lori Jahns to Rochester High. They were rival cheerleaders.

But Madonna had solo-flirtation and going-steady rights with big-smiling Nick Twomey who is now a Michigan pastor. And she developed her forever fascination with Marilyn Monroe turning herself into a Monroe Wanna Be.

THREE

SEXUAL ADVENTURES

'The only remotely entertainment-orientated

dream I ever had was one where I dreamed I kissed

Robert Redford. I was in the sixth grade. And it

has not come true.'

MADONNA IN 1990

The Revd Nick Twomey is a neatly dressed, dark-haired man with horn-rimmed glasses, a picture of propriety. He is pastor at the Faith Reformed Church in Traverse City, Michigan. He used to 'go steady' with Madonna and they were friends until they both graduated from Rochester-Adams High School in 1976. She was a cheerleader. He played on the football, basketball and baseball teams. 'We did some serious flirting. We sort of hung out together,' recalled the pastor. 'You do that more, I suppose, than going steady in seventh, eighth and ninth grade.'

Neither of them belonged in the popular, mainstream crowd at school. He became a Christian. She took on her 'European look'. They were different.

Even when we were no longer super close, we had mutual respect for one another because neither of us cared what the other kids thought. My life zigged, her life zagged.

We've all heard about her rebel life, but I'm not so sure she was *such* a rebel. Neither of us had halos on our heads, but I don't know that either one of us was any worse than the other.

I've thought about Madonna and I remember how she was. She was often confused. I wonder if she is happy. I suspect that underneath all the fame and fortune is a person in need of love, forgiveness and hope.

In her teens she was misunderstood. The boys would call her 'a nympho' and the girls put her down as 'a slut'. She was still a virgin. She was never one to wait to be asked for a date. If she liked a boy, she asked him out. She got a reputation. She was necking with the boys. And there was some heavy petting. She took precautions: to heavy necking parties, what they called 'make-out' nights, she wore a turtle-necked blue bodysuit. No matter how hot it got, there were several zippers between her virginity and lusty teenaged boys. But teenagers, those hormones on two legs, are on a constant sexual voyage of discovery. She could not go on forever being the girl who went to church every Sunday morning in a starched-white dress and who knelt with her brothers and sisters, father and stepmother in the third row from front at Sunday best.

She lost her virginity in the back of a Cadillac. Later, she would regret describing it – in a joke that backfired – as a career move. But she did not go 'all the way' until she had been dating Russell Long, who was two years older and drove that infamous Cadillac for several months. 'I don't know if it was anything to do with me,' says Russell. 'I think it was more to do with adventure, of the experience of the unknown. She really wanted to find out what it was like.'

Sex was now very much on her mind. She and Carol Belanger would joke about it – they even stripped Ken and Barbie and put them face-to-face under the covers of Barbie's bed. Madonna spent hours reading *Glamour* and *Seventeen* magazines. They gave her the sweater idea, a way to brighten up her school uniform by wearing hot pink, purple and orange sweaters. She was never frightened of others laughing at her or jeering at her. Most of us do not like to be stared at for being different, the odd one out. Madonna's strength in the playground – and now – is that she does not care what others think. She says she knew she was different from the age of five. So, having her first sexual experience was not because of peer pressure: it was simply because she wanted to see what it was like. She was fifteen. Now, 'the idea that the first guy I ever slept with is married and has kids really breaks me up. I wonder if he still loves me – he probably does.'

But there were sexual adventures before that. In her 1991 documentary, *Truth or Dare* (released in Britain under the title *In Bed With Madonna*), Madonna would confront the woman she says 'finger-fucked' her when they both lived in Michigan. The woman in question could not recall the particular incident. Madonna counters: 'All children experiment with each other sexually when they're little. These are things that people just want to sweep under the rug and treat like dark, dirty secrets, when they shouldn't be.' And Madonna says that from her earliest sexual longings, she was attracted to *all* sides of sexuality. As with everything else in her life, she wanted to know *all* about it.

In those growing-up years, Madonna felt great pressure to 'fit in', to be part of a group. You had to be a member of the church, a participant in neighbourhood and school activities. That pressure made her angry. The escape was to dance to Motown records at her friends' homes. They would stack portable turn-tables with 45s – the Supremes, Martha and the Vandellas, the Shirelles, the Ronettes – and dance and sing. Ooooooohhh, baby love and be-bop-de-bop. She made up routines. The other kids would give her standing ovations and she liked the applause. The other pastime was to go to what today we would call an 'art' cinema – one that showed foreign and old movies. She saw flickering black and whites with Carole Lombard and Judy Holliday. And Bardot and Marilyn Monroe – 'She was my first movie idol. When I first saw her, I wanted to make my hair blonde and wear pointy bras.'

Madonna saw herself in those screen sirens. Her humour, her need to be the boss, to be in control and at the same time be cared for. She was then the paradox she is today. She had knowledge. She also had innocence. And years later, in December 1986, she would pose Monroe-style in the pages of *Life* magazine. And she did it again, even more spectacularly, on the cover and pages of Italian *Vogue* and world-wide editions of *Vanity Fair* in March 1991. She had 'become' Marilyn for the camera. She posed and pouted like her idol and a few weeks later appeared at a Beverly Hills benefit concert in a short, black dress – a mirror of Monroe.

Psychologists have warned her about this obsession. But she believes Monroe, whose mother was committed to an asylum soon after Monroe was born, rose above her difficult start in life. She is irritated when warned off the Monroe reincarnate track: 'Marilyn Monroe was a victim and I'm not. I know what I'm doing and what I want. If I make mistakes or fall into traps, they're mine, not Marilyn Monroe's.'

She has a collection of Monroe memorabilia. In the videos for 'Material Girl' and 'Papa Don't Preach' she struts Monroe-style recalling her idol's hit films, *Gentlemen Prefer Blondes* and *There's No Business Like Showbusiness*. She shrugs off stories that she consulted psychics who told her she was Monroe reincarnate. But it is a subject she has pursued since her mid-teens.

She was the one to call on for a different take. At junior high school, classmate Jonathan Gilbert decided to make a short 8mm film. For his cameras, he wanted a naked tummy on which to simulate frying an egg. Madonna obliged.

By sixteen, dance had become her passion. Whenever touring dance companies visited the Detroit area, she would fight for tickets. She took every dance class she could. It was then that her teenaged anger subdued. She had orientated herself: 'I was a little girl from Michigan and I had a dream and I worked really hard and my dream came true,' She wanted to dance seriously. And Christopher Flynn taught serious dance.

Flynn was forty-five, a lean man with thinning hair and glasses, when Madonna met him. He was a homosexual and a

Catholic. She adored him. Her family was not in the least worldly and Michigan is not America's most cultural state. It is a hard-working, blue-collar place, and no more so than Detroit and its suburbs. Flynn understood Madonna. She looked to him as a mentor, a father-figure and even as an imaginary lover and brother. Lover, brother and father – a trinity of people the seventeen-year-old felt she did not have close to her. Flynn did not disguise his sexual preference. Instead, he took Madonna to gay discothèques in downtown Detroit. The crowd was swallowing 'poppers' (capsules of amyl nitrate) and talking literature and poetry. They could not be more different from all those school playground jocks whose lives revolved around sports, drinking and girls. This was glamour. This was sophistication. What it was, of course, was new and different. He took her to museums and art exhibitions in Detroit. And they would go dancing, which Flynn was later to recall:

She was hot. People would clear the floor. But she's that way about life. She was always trying to be better, always positive, always filled with urgency, always wanting the most of it and she had this tremendous thirst for everything. She was insatiable.

Even for silly knock-knock-who's-there jokes. Flynn remembered a two-hour drive in which she made them up one after the other, after the other and he marvelled: 'They were good.'

Madonna had graduated from Rochester High and won a dance scholarship at the University of Michigan, an achievement that had not thrilled her father. By then she wore her hair in a short, spiky punk look. There was discipline including a tough *plié* exercise – low knee bends with the stomach held tightly in and the posture perfect. Madonna broke the class up one day during the exercise with a loud belch. On a hot day she wanted to take off her leotards and just wear a bra, no knickers. She hammed it up in ballet class. She ripped pieces out of her leotards and wore safety pins and scratched runs into her tights.

Flynn had told her she had a face like a Roman statue. She was extremely well built for her age with breasts that had the neighbourhood boys goggle-eyed – something she did nothing to discourage. But Flynn told her she was beautiful. No one had said that before. Even Russell in his moments of passion had praised her body rather than her total look. She understood Flynn to mean that she was beautiful not only in appearance but inside. It was then that her mind took that step further on from fact, on to theory and later to the fantasies she would captalize on in her career. Anything was possible.

Madonna has no doubts about Flynn's influence:

I'd say that after my father, the most powerful, important relationship of my life was with Christopher Flynn. I didn't understand the concept of gay at that time. I was probably twelve or thirteen years old. All I knew was that my ballet teacher was different from everybody else. He was so alive. He had a certain theatricality about him. He made you proud of yourself, just the way he came up to me and put my face in his hand and said, 'You are beautiful.' No one had woken up that part of me yet. I was too busy being repressed by my Catholic father.

By the time I was fifteen or sixteen, he took me to my first gay club to go dancing. I'd never been to a club. I'd only been to high-school dances, and no guys would ever ask me to dance, because they thought I was insane, so I'd just go out and dance by myself.

Flynn's gay world made her feel 'normal'. And she explains:

In school and in my neighbourhood and everything, I felt like such an outsider, a misfit, a weirdo. And suddenly, when I went to the gay club, I didn't feel that way anymore. I just felt at home. I had a whole new sense of myself.

Until that point, I kept seeing myself through macho, heterosexual eyes. Because I was a really aggressive woman, guys thought of me as a really strange girl. I know I frightened them. I didn't add up for them. They didn't want to ask me out. I felt inadequate around them, and I felt not beautiful, and I felt like I could never fit in with the prom queens and the cheerleaders and the perfect girls that all went out with the football players.

You can understand Flynn's attraction for this 'misfit'.

I was really down on myself. When Christopher introduced me to this life, I suddenly thought, *That's not the only way that I have to be.* I felt that my behaviour was accepted around him. My father didn't know. At the time, he would have freaked out.

People didn't talk about gay life in the Catholic Church. They barely talked about sex. So I didn't see it as something I was supposed to be wary of or afraid of. All I knew was, I was attracted to Christopher and his lifestyle. I fell in love with him and the way he treated me. I started spending a lot of time with dancers, and almost every male dancer that I knew was gay. Then I went through another kind of feeling inadequate because I was constantly falling in love with gay men. Of course, I was so miserable that I wasn't a man.

But she had the 'balls' to move on.

It was Flynn who encouraged Madonna to stretch, to move away, to try New York. Flynn died of AIDS at the Hernandez House hospice in Los Angeles on 27 October 1990. Madonna was distraught. A California newspaper contacted Flynn a few weeks before he died. He told them that he and Madonna had kept in touch: 'We still remained friends after Madonna found her own way in life and achieved her dream. We had a special relationship. She was a very worldly sort of woman even when she was little more than a child.'

Flynn had told her New York. She told her father. He was against it. So was just about everybody else. But Flynn had told her she was beautiful, she could do it. She felt she was simply marking time at the University of Michigan Dance Department, just tuning her technique. She dropped out and took a Northwest Airlines jet – her first plane ride – to New York. Her ticket cost her $88.

FOUR

CHEAP POPCORN

'I always meet certain people at certain times

in my life who can help me'

MADONNA IN 1985

Michigan to Manhattan? It is a lot longer than the miles involved. Madonna was nearly nineteen. And budding. There was no hiding her figure – and she did not try. And she did not have any thoughts about the perils of the big city. She was totally self-absorbed and hardly noticed the passengers on the jet. She was the one heading for New York City and the big time. If there were any regrets about her leaving her hometown, they belonged to Steve Bray. Some months earlier at the smoke-filled, Blue Frogge nightclub, a favourite of the University of Michigan's preppy crowd, she had picked him up. She had been dancing up a storm and fighting off the attention of a crowd of students when Bray caught her eye. He was black. He was a waiter. He was also funny. And more importantly – he was cool. Bray was also a gifted

35

musician, a drummer with a local band that worked the Detroit lounge circuit. Bray – like so many in the years to come – was captivated by Madonna's energy and what he would later call her 'aura of ambition'. And it was that insensitive ambition which allowed her to leave Steve Bray – a man who would later have an enormous impact on her life and career – at home barely realizing his feelings for her.

It was midsummer when Madonna landed at La Guardia Airport. Hot and sticky. She was carrying the dark-blue winter coat which she could not fit into her suitcase which held her ballet shoes, tights, underwear, a couple of outfit changes, two pairs of street shoes, and a picture of her mother, Madonna. She gathered her belongings together and, weighed down by her case, staggered down the escalator and through the glass electric doors to the yellow-cab rank outside La Guardia's Northwest terminal. She told the cab driver to take her to the middle of everything.

She was lucky. The driver took her to Times Square and only wanted a dozen dollars for the trip. She walked east on 42nd Street and then south on Lexington Avenue. There was one of those open-air summer markets going on Lexington. By now she was wearing her coat rather than carrying it. A man started following her. It looked as though all her father's predictions about coming to a nasty end in New York were coming true faster than even he could have believed. But he was no rapist or mugger – rather, a Good Samaritan. He quizzed her about why she was wearing a coat in the heat. She explained she was just off the plane and had nowhere to stay.

She stayed at his apartment for her first two weeks in New York with breakfast provided. He showed her the city and then she was off, in one cockroach-infested slum after another. She would try to eat one apple a day, but mainly lived on popcorn. It was cheap. It filled her up. She also dined out of street rubbish bins. She would look for the McDonald's bags because there were usually a few french fries in them. She was also adept at 'borrowing' five dollars from every other man she met. She was sexually ambivalent to these men, come hither but go no further. 'She was definitely not trampy, not free with her sexual favours,' says Camille Barbone who was Madonna's first manager and mentor. 'She never lost her sense of pride. She always carried herself with a great deal of dignity.'

She spent a long time living in a rooming house on 30th Street between 8th and 9th Avenue. Steve Bray and other friends recall the stench: vagrants peed or did worse in doorways. She moved up to a place between Avenues A and B and Bray, a gregarious, round-faced and friendly character, says the smell was better but when he visited, 'I always thought I was going to be killed by junkies.'

New York, New York. Madonna gritted her teeth. She was a cloakroom girl at the trendy Russian Tea Room on West 57th. She was lonely. But there was nowhere else to go. She could not go home, could she? That would be defeat. She went to work for Dunkin' Donuts which had a less jet-set crowd than the Tea Room. She left after a disagreement with an overbearing customer. She could not drive (she got a California licence in 1985 after a back-to-back series of lessons) but she would dress up and just wander around the city with people gaping at her outlandish outfits. She would ride the subway enjoying all the attention. The Lower East Side of New York was her territory.

She got a job slinging food at a Burger King fast-food outlet just down from Central Park. The pay was $1.50 an hour. Over at art classes they paid $10 an hour for nude modelling. She suddenly felt – financially and emotionally – rampantly artistic. Her body was in great shape, if a little underweight, from her popcorn diet. Her muscle definition and skeleton were on display for the student artists. She was their favourite model – she was easy to draw. She started modelling privately in people's homes. And that involved photographers. Her attitude was that Michelangelo was not a pornographer and neither were the artists and photographers she posed for.

And there were many, many modelling sessions from 1979 to 1980, but the truth of it was that they were more to put food on the table and pay the rent than for the artistic endeavour. Later, of course, like Marilyn Monroe before her, the nudes would surface after she became a world-wide phenomenon.

It is now hot stuff. Back then it was cold work. 'It was cold in my studio,' remembers photographer, Martin Schreiber. 'I had two heaters on Madonna but she was laughing.' Schreiber founded the Photographing the Nude course at New York's New School. From 10 February through Valentine's Day in 1979 his students snapped away at a new model whom their teacher called 'a beautiful, intelligent, unconventional lady'. He says now:

She was skinnier. There was something special about her that's for sure. I think she's quite beautiful now, but she had a different kind of beauty then. I don't think she really knew what she wanted then but she had some ideas.

She was experimenting. She would do whatever it took to get to where she wanted to go.

Of the photographic sessions he said:

There was no hesitation on her part. 'Here I am – it's no big deal,' that was her attitude. With lots of nudes I don't photograph faces, but with her I wanted to include the face. Madonna had *such* a face. The nudes I've done are lovely. There's something wonderful in a beautiful form that happens to be somebody's body. One of my roles is to make people look at nudes differently. I'm trying to make people feel less uptight about their bodies because we're living in a puritanical age.

He said that his students had to pay cash to Madonna for modelling: she couldn't take cheques because she did not have a bank account.

Lee Friedlander, who was awarded a Medal of Paris in 1981 and has three Guggenheim fellowships, says of model Madonna:

I was curious to try my hand at the nude. She seemed a very confident and street-wise girl. She told me she was putting a band together, but half the kids that age are doing that. She was a good professional model.

The Friedlander and Schreiber photographs reveal Madonna still in her 'European mood'. Her armpits are unshaven. Her hair is dark and curled. In some pictures she is pouting, in others she looks pensive. In one she stares warily at the camera.

As well she might have. By the time she was a pop sensation, her naked body was stapled all over the pages of *Playboy* and

Penthouse magazines. The black and white nudes of the $10-an-hour (sometimes cut rate to $7-an-hour) model had sold for more than $100,000 to *Playboy*. But Schreiber and Friedlander revealed that their picture sessions with Madonna, which were published in *Playboy* in 1985, were a 'job lot'. They paid her only $25.

She did a little better from photographer, Bill Stone, who sold his pictures – he will not say for how much – to *Penthouse* magazine.

I was going to write her a cheque, but she wanted cash [recalls Stone]. I fished in my pockets for all the money I had and it was $50. She said, 'I can't take that much money.' As she was leaving she said, 'I can't take all of your money – take some back.' And she handed me a few dollars.

Others were also cashing in on Madonna's modelling days. Madonna had attracted many people during her months in New York. One was Stephen Lewicki who persuaded the nineteen-year-old to appear in *A Certain Sacrifice*, a soft-porn exercise which is guilty of being both exploitative and boring. You have to think if Madonna had made a porno movie it would at least not be boring. In the film she is involved in a rape scene in a coffee shop, an orgiastic dance session and a ritual sacrifice. *High Society* magazine paid out $100,000 for out-take nudes of Madonna from the film. She had been paid $100 to appear in the movie. (Madonna later sued Lewicki to stop him using her name when he released the film – Madonna nude suddenly made this sex-slave toss a marketing possibility in 1985.)

Madonna brazened out the nude pictures. But they did get to her:

At first, the *Playboy* pictures were hurtful to me and I wasn't sure how I felt about them. Now I look back at them and feel silly that I ever got upset, but I did want to keep some things private. It's like when you're a little girl at school and some nun comes and lifts up your dress in front of everybody and you get really embarrassed; it's not a real terrible thing in the end but you're not ready for it. It seems so awful and you seem so exposed. It's other people's problem if they turn them into something smutty. That was never my intention.

Back in 1980 her dream of stardom was still that. It was time
for Little Orphan Annie to meet Mae West. Another example, as
Miss West would have surely said, of goodness having nothing to
do with it. It was literally the time for flash/trash. Her desperation
showed in her choice of outfits – she was hanging out in New York
bars wearing little more than her underwear. She craved attention. There are the tales of her scholarship with the famed Alvin
Ailey American Dance Theatre, but they are just stories. She was
asked to work with the Theatre's third company, which is much
like being in the reserves.

What she quickly found out was that she was not the only
ambitious girl in New York. It was like being in the movie *Fame* –
everyone could sing and dance and wanted a break. Madonna,
spiking her hair, tearing her leotards and being different, lasted
for thirteen weeks at the Dance Theatre before she went to train
with Pearl Lang who was a protégé of dance-legend, Martha
Graham. Madonna's father came to visit. Her apartment at 232
East 4th Street was cockroach city. Silvio Ciccone pleaded. His
daughter told him fame and fortune were just around the corner.
But not quite the next corner. There were still many hurdles.
Madonna and Pearl Lang did not agree about training methods
and they split up. It was time for change personally as well.

She was still taking dance classes. She was also partying – and
at a party she met Dan Gilroy. Gilroy was here, there and also
renting an abandoned synagogue in Corona, Queens. He and his
brother, Ed, lived and rehearsed there. They were musicians.
They were also Madonna's passport out of the cockroach gulch.
She moved in with them.

'She never really liked modelling,' says Gilroy who favours
jeans, sneakers and plaid shirts.

She would come home and complain about it sometimes or she would talk
about how some photographer had tried to come on to her. She posed for me
too. I did paintings and sketches but she didn't like staying in position so I'd
let her read and relax when I was painting. She made better money modelling than any other job she could get.

Madonna was beautiful and alive and wanted to be a star. She'd wake up every morning, a quick cup of coffee and get right on the phone calling her contacts, getting her career moving. She'd call anywhere and everyone. She worked hard. She learned to play drums with us. She'd practice five hours a day. She was a dancer and she had a sense of the beat. We got to be very close. We were living in the basement of the synagogue and using its large meeting room as a rehearsal and recording studio. My brother Ed and a beautiful blonde girl named Angie Smit were also in the band. We were pretty good but the gigs just weren't there. We might get one or two paying jobs a month and if you got $80 a night, that was a lot. And we were dividing the money four ways.

She modelled once or twice a week. Sometimes she enjoyed the sessions if the photographer or artist was very good and professional. Once she gave me some beautiful nude photos that she was very proud of. She even wrote a little Chinese poem on a card attached to the pictures. It talked about how some people want women to have bound feet but others want women whose feet are free. I think that maybe it was her way of saying she was free and liberated.

Madonna would go to the corner market and bargain with the counter men for the best vegetables and fruit she could get for the money. One time we were on hands and knees looking for loose change to buy a few potatoes. We had fun too. We'd go dancing, but only on week nights when it wasn't too crowded and we could really move around the floor. Our only luxuries were bicycles. Madonna was young. She was influenced by the people around her. When we played our gigs, Angie dressed really sexy with see-through clothes and she moved sensuously on stage. And Madonna began to do these things too. She was dark-haired then, but she saw Angie's long blonde hair got the attention when she was on stage. Maybe that contributed to her finally going blonde.

Gilroy and Madonna and the band they called the Breakfast Club stayed together for a little more than a year. If things had gone differently in Europe, it might have been more a matter of days. Madonna has always taken every opportunity. Back then, she had little thought about anything but advancement.

Patrick Hernandez was a discothèque pin-up, all movement and not too much substance. He had success with a disco drivel titled, 'Born To Be Alive'. Madonna was offered a job dancing and singing back-up for him. In Paris. Paris, France, that is. She was on Cloud Nine. Seventh Heaven. She squeaked her delight to anyone who would listen. Michigan to Manhattan. And now April in Paris? *D'accord, cherie.*

FIVE

THE DEAL

'You have to work for something. If it's handed to you, it's not gonna last.'

MADONNA IN 1987

━━━━━━

The Eiffel Tower. The Champs-Elysées. The city where a young girl's thoughts turn to ... misery and loneliness. In Paris she had an apartment, a maid and a voice coach. Producers Jean Claude Pellerin and Jean Van Lieu, the Two Jeans, said they would make her the new Edith Piaf. Like so many before her, Madonna was to hear the immortal words: 'We want to make you a star.' It was a Pygmalion fantasy for the Frenchmen who had brought Hernandez's act to France. Now they could work on Madonna. But she was no fair lady. She wanted to work, to sing and dance, and not be touted around town as an upwardly mobile urchin. She had picked up enough French to get the drift of the pitch from the Two Jeans.

Madonna reacted quite typically. She rebelled. If they wanted

---

her to be at a certain restaurant she would be out and about with a Vietnamese boyfriend who had an enormous asset – a motorcycle for scooting through the Paris traffic. When she went on tour with Hernandez to Tunisia, she was more enthusiastic about the night-clubs than his act. During the stay she went swimming. In a one-piece body stocking. She stuck out on the beach. Back in Paris she would order a string of desserts in very proper restaurants just to embarrass her hosts. This was not the France of Bardot and the films she saw in Rochester. She was all but dismissed and no one talked to her in English.

She was annoyed and upset to the degree her personality dictated – mad as hell. She was an ornament, not the star ornament, not the star of this particular road show. And she did not like it. The Two Jeans gave her money to keep her quiet. They introduced her to French boys, whom she liked – with their trim hips and interest in fashion. The more effeminate the men she met, the more intrigued she was. She feels the same today:

I see them as my *alter egos*. I feel very drawn to them. I think like a guy but I'm feminine. I relate to feminine men. When I was in the ballet world, I wished I was a boy because I just wanted *somebody* to ask me out. Actually it would be great to be both sexes.

Jean Claude Pellerin's wife, Michèlle, recalls Madonna's impact on the men of Paris, the pot-bellied and the slim-hipped:

She stayed with me and my husband in Paris. She was very beautiful and she dated a lot of French boys. She thought they were very old-fashioned and she was very free. Very free and very liberal. She wanted a lot of boys. She liked the attention.

But she *really* only wanted to be one thing – to be a star. And when she left Paris she promised me she would come back as a star.

Of course, she kept the promise. She returned a star, but in her individual way as always. She distracted the catwalk models at 1991's spring fashion show by wandering around in short skirts that often revealed she was wearing no underwear.

Madonna had spent five indulgent months in Paris. However, her French mentors had flopped at their attempt to pull off a Professor Higgins double-act. It was that young man back in

Queens, New York, in the rented synagogue, who was to provide the initial spark for the Madonna magic. Dan Gilroy had kept up a steady stream of letters to Madonna. 'We miss you. You must return to America.' She did, driven back by frustration, and a disabling attack of pneumonia. She called the synagogue from Kennedy Airport. She was back on stage with the Breakfast Club.

Madonna and the Gilroy brothers and Angie Smit made beautiful music together. It was a free-wheeling time and Madonna felt the happiest she had ever been in her life. She felt loved. She felt wanted. And needed. She was writing songs now, and not just playing the drums, but any instrument that Dan or Ed Gilroy would help her with. Madonna had the business brain. She was also the 'balls' of the group as the others recall it. She went about trying to set up appearances, record deals: 'I think I was just naturally more charming to those horny old businessmen than Dan and Ed Gilroy.' From her earliest days with Daddy, she had known how to twist men to her point of view.

And there was always fear. A morbid fear of death ever since her mother died. Madonna had lived longer than her mother. What about Marilyn? She died at thirty-six. She thinks about that now. But there was no fear in jetting in from Michigan, suburban street-smart but still Manhattan naïve: she was a ripe, well-built cherry, parachuting blind into Times Square, the Big Apples' rotten core of pornography and drugs and prostitution and any which way combination of all of them. There was no fear in going to Paris and literally living off the kindness of strangers.

But deep inside herself there was an irrational fear. Of failure. Of being alone. Of dying. Most of us share some of these fears but most also tend to shove on through them and get on with living. She fed off her fear. It was the catalyst, the blue touch-paper for her unique and exceptional career which was about to explode like a fireworks display. There were some flying sparks to deal with first. She was not fearful about them.

The Gilroys had been trying to make it for five years. They

knew their music. Madonna's motto was: 'What do you know? Teach it to me.' She was pushing and pushing hard, and later it would sound harsh when she talked about those particular early days: 'I took advantage of the situation. I wanted to know everything they knew because I could make it work for my benefit.'

Gilroy found himself something of a Dr Frankenstein. He had created a problem: Madonna wanted to sing in the band; the band already had a singer. He was torn between his loyalty to his brother Ed and to Madonna who also wanted to sing her own songs. She had turned into a monster for Dan Gilroy.

She was fun, you know. But I knew that with that kind of drive and devotion to getting ahead something had to happen. I don't know if she was more talented than the rest of the group. More driven, and an incredible attention getter. It was fun. It was a good year.

The romance, the learning and her role with the Breakfast Club was over. She left the synagogue. Queens was dead. Long live the big city.

Back in Manhattan, she called on the contacts she had established. She rapped her knuckles on record-company doors. There were boyfriends, one for Sunday, Monday, Tuesday, and so on and – if she didn't get confused – it would all work out on Saturday night. One man invited to a party asked if he could bring a date and was told 'Sure, bring a date. We can *all* do something.'

But Camille Barbone still says all the boyfriends did not mean a roundabout of sex. It was contacts.

She called herself a Boy Toy, but in no way was she a career prostitute. She didn't have to be. Madonna is a sexual creature who has men eating out of her hands. She knows about timing. A simple word like 'Hi' delivered by Madonna and men are reduced to stuttering and stammering. She had men lending her money and musicians rehearsing and giving their time without pay – and she wasn't sleeping with any of them.

She was sleeping in New York's garment centre in a twelve-storey structure called the Music Building simply because it had been converted into a series of rehearsal rooms. Madonna was still scrounging food on the streets – and accommodations in the building. When the last group left the place, she snuggled down for the night. In the morning, before the first group arrived she would use the basic toilet facilities.

Madonna took pride in making do. People could not understand how she lived. The popcorn. The daily apple. The bought meal. The borrowed five bucks. She was feeding on fear. And she was ravenous.

Around the New York clubs, she was known as a bit of a 'prick teaser'. A pragmatic one. After she got things – shall we say stimulated? – she got her way but those stimulated did not necessarily get theirs. But for most men it did not matter. It was a turn on, a thrill. She was funny. Rude. Terrific to look at. Sexy. Fun to be with. She was an all-round entertainer. A dangerous and different one. Because you never knew what you were going to get. It is the same today. She frightens. She fascinates.

Back in New York, she was more interested in being fascinating. Again, fate blessed her. Steve Bray, the tall, pony-tailed waiter from the Blue Frogge in Detroit called. She needed a drummer. He was in New York in six days. He brought some musical know-how and 'cool' to the motley band Madonna had gathered around her.

Bray moved in with her in the Music Building. He sensed Madonna was not held in the greatest awe by the crowd who used the rehearsal halls.

I think there was a lot of resentment of someone who has obviously got that special something. There are so many musicians out there, but there are only a few who really have that charisma. That community frowned on her. She had trouble making friends.

It was like a commune. Madonna was not a commune person. She was a Madonna person. A solo act. She wanted to call the group 'Madonna'. The self-effacing Bray told her that was an upsetting idea. So, they called themselves the Millionaires (bottom dollar as it turned out) and then Modern Dance (no one stepped out to them) and Emmy (a nickname Dan Gilroy had given Madonna, but still did not bring good luck). She made a demo tape. Camille Barbone heard it. She was managing rock bands around the city at the time. A deal was done. Madonna, for the first time in her life, was on salary. She knew how to spend. Outtttaaahere! was the cry. The Music Building was history. She moved to New York's Upper West Side. Steve Bray moved uptown too.

Her new band was called 'Madonna'. Camille Barbone had been promised old-fashioned rock 'n roll. Madonna wanted funk, funk and funkier. There were shouting matches. Madonna went with rock 'n roll but she was, as always, influenced by those closest to her. They wanted to be cool. Even cooler. All day she would write the songs that they wanted with Steve Bray and at the clubs they would play the music the management – both their own and the club's – wanted.

They would play the Roxy. Or the Danceteria. Which was where Mark Kamins changed Madonna's life. Well-connected, in many senses, Kamins was a disc jockey who mattered. And his Saturday-night crowd liked to impress him. For Kamins his popularity meant less lonely nights at home. At Danceteria, he was a star and he had his groupies. He came on to Madonna. She flirted right back. She got what she wanted. Kamins listened to the demonstration recording made by Madonna and Steve Bray which included a song called 'Everybody'. Kamins adored it. It became one of the specials at Danceteria. The kids danced to it – they had to. Kamins recalls: 'Everybody going to night-clubs has other ambitions, but she was special.'

So special that Kamins helped finance a re-recording of that demonstration tape. And negotiated – solo – a deal for her with Sire Records. It was a *big* rung on the ladder.

Steve Bray was beside himself. He would produce Madonna's first album. Kamins was hopelessly happy. He would produce Madonna's first record. Wrong. Both of them. Madonna was scared. She felt she had been handed a golden egg – and she wanted it hatched by experts.

SIX

THE EXPERTS

'Even when I was a little girl I knew I wanted the whole world to know who I was, to love me and be affected by me.'

MADONNA IN 1985

The challenge of channelling Madonna's enormous but often erratic energy into her first album went to Reggie Lucas who had previously produced for Stephanie Mills and Roberta Flack. It happened in a roundabout way after Madonna had put herself in a position of being an investment worth hundreds of thousands of dollars. And it followed much Madonna-manipulation behind the scenes. Both Mark Kamins and Steve Bray had their hopes, but Madonna had her own dreams and also her own way of pursuing them at the Danceteria, the four floors of the Chelsea discothèque that offered funky music and hospitality to a crowd who favoured skin-tight leather and purple hair – anything exotic, but always different. Mark Kamins had contacted Michael Rosenblatt, a music-world talent scout who worked for Sire

Records, the 'New Wave' arm of the giant Warner Brothers Communication Group.

Rosenblatt caught what amounted to performances by Madonna at the Danceteria. These were the days of the belly-button look. Madonna wore jangles of jewellery (she got it free from Maripol, a French designer who was on the scene) and every piece of clothing had a suggestive rip or tear. Some of the Danceteria crowd say that at times Madonna looked as though she had been through a spin dryer attached to her 'BOY TOY' belt. Not everyone got the humour. When she was living in the East Village, her hangout was the Roxy. It was full of graffiti artists and break dancers. All of them had nicknames which they would write on the club walls. There would be 'Hi-Fi' or 'Whiz-Kid'. The game was to see how many times you could get this tag name up on the wall. The slang was you 'threw up' your name on the walls. Madonna 'threw up' her 'BOY TOY'. The crowd thought it was hilarious. Madonna saw it as a tongue-in-cheek statement, the opposite of what was meant. She was not available to anyone – but outside of the Roxy no one knew that. The controversy was beginning, the slut label that had haunted her school-days was back again. Madonna resents that. And the talk that she slept her way to success. Sure, she learned music from a string of guys, some of whom she had sex with. It is not that she was annoyed at the suggestion she used sex to get where she wanted – just furious that anyone thought Madonna could not get there simply on her own talent and drive. That was what was insulting. And it was later the sexual promiscuity of some of her partners rather than her own which convinced her to take a test for AIDS. The result was negative.

Such scary thoughts were not in the atmosphere of the Danceteria where Madonna's ambition and plotting were about to get her the result she so desperately wanted. When Rosenblatt saw her at the Danceteria, he scented 'a find' and a big-dollar one at that. He remembers that when he first saw Madonna at the disco club he thought two things: she looked wild and she looked beautiful. On stage she danced to Kamins' re-recording of her doing 'Everybody'. The word was being passed around the right circles, and a deal was about to go down.

Seymour Stein was in Lennox Hill Hospital, New York, suffering from heart problems. As the boss of Sire Records, he had to finalize any recording deal with Madonna. A stocky man with what hair he has left worn in tight, grey curls, Stein is a music mogul. He got to the top spotting talent and trends. The buzz on Madonna was so strong he agreed to meet her in his hospital room. He shaved, combed his hair and bought a new dressing gown for the meeting. The nurses told him not to get so excited, to watch the stress. When Madonna arrived, he had forgotten all about his dressing gown. He had a drop feed in his left arm and was sitting by his bed wearing his underpants.

It was a strange but, with hindsight, totally appropriate beginning for the Material Girl's career. Stein, although impressed by Madonna's tape which he had played on one of the giant 'portable' stereos in his hospital room, was still the wily businessman. He committed – but just so much. Madonna would be paid $5000 as an advance for a contract to make three singles.

It was Easter 1982 when she went into a recording studio to remake 'Everybody'. The record was showcased at the Danceteria – and what a showcase. She got three dancers – one of them a gay artist, Martin Burgoyne, whom she had roomed with before trying to get enough money to buy lunch with the Breakfast Club – and they put on a sensational act. It was raunchy. It was sexy. It was sensational. It blazed out dollar signs. In neon. Seymour Stein was there to watch her. So were Steve Bray and Mark Kamins.

Fans said she sounded 'black'. She was not pictured on her record covers. It was only when she appeared in public they realized this 5 ft. 4 in. tall Italian-American was pounding the sound out. The irony of these appearances was that she was asked to lip-synch to her record and getting paid more than when she had performed properly. She was being heard in gay clubs. Black clubs. Transvestite bars. Rock clubs. Every place they were making music. Her next record 'Burning Up' – again a 12-inch disco single

– was put out and with it a cheaply made video (unlike the more sophisticated and sometimes controversial videos which followed).

She moped for some moments then bounced back. Like a jellybean. She likes smooth skin, lips and the Latin look in her men. Enter John Benitez, a.k.a 'Jellybean' Benitez: 'She didn't bowl me over at first. Then we started holding hands and buying each other little presents.' They became a solid item – she even took him home to Rochester. Her father approved of Jellybean more than his daughter's outlandish all-black outfit worn for Thanksgiving dinner. Now a respected producer, Jellybean was the resident disc jockey at the Funland discothèque when he met Madonna. Now, he makes his own music. They remain very close. Interestingly, he says their first couple of years together were glued by mutual ambition: 'We both started to move at the same pace. We're both very career orientated, very goal orientated. We both wanted to be stars.' And Madonna never more so that when Sire Records told her that they were prepared to bankroll an album.

She turned her back on Bray and Kamins. It was a bitter falling out with Bray who told Madonna she had no ethics. 'It was very hard to accept,' he says. But he had no choice. He joined Dan Gilroy and the Breakfast Club, another crowd Madonna had left behind. Kamins was in the same position.

'Sure, I was hurt,' he says. 'At the time, I felt stepped on. But I don't think there's a mean bone in her body. Maybe a mean knuckle, but not a mean bone.'

Maybe not mean. But tough.

All my boyfriends turned out to be helpful to my career. That's not the reason I stayed with them. I loved them all very much. I'm not Alexis from *Dynasty*. All the men I stepped over to get to the top – all of them would have me back because they all still love me and I love them.

Professionally, the man who really mattered at that moment was record producer Reggie Lucas. He did not last long. The album *Madonna* was released in America in July 1983. The first single from it was 'Holiday', a song which had been brought to her by Jellybean. Everyone had enormous hopes for it, but it made a minor splash. Later, there were radio plays of 'Borderline' and 'Lucky Star'. They were on the record charts.

What was to make Madonna was her first video; quickly followed by a second. This was the breakthrough. Her dance background, her sense of the outrageous and her songs all blended together for the MTV generation. She just knew how to 'come across' sexually and later explained: 'I've been in touch with that aspect of my personality since I was five.'

Madonna had given Reggie Lucas the go-ahead for the 'sound' of her début album, but she did not go for the finished product. It was not her. Too sharp, too sleek. Impersonal. She felt she was as good a judge as these professional producers. And she told them so.

Lucas recalls:

I wanted to push her in a pop direction. She was a little more orientated toward the disco thing, but I thought she had appeal to the general market. It's funny about the thing with Kamins and Bray. The same thing that happened to them pretty much happened to me on her second record when they had Nile Rodgers.

Lucas was dropped from the Madonna express. Madonna went after Rodgers who had worked with David Bowie and Duran Duran for her *Like a Virgin* album.

Madonna was on the move – literally. In 1983 she had gone to London to promote 'Everybody' and appeared at the Camden Palace club, where a couple years earlier she had met the then top of the pops, Boy George. Madonna did not even believe he had a group. All she remembered was he wore high heels and was surrounded by men dressed just like him. She was intrigued. She liked everything feminine. But she was not in control of this particular adrogony and she did not hang around to watch the action.

Even a year after the release of her first album, which was dedicated to Silvio Ciccone, she was not really a 'name' outside of the New York club circuit. She could go to the Danceteria – a Class of '82 type reunion – and not be mobbed. Or 'throw-up' with the boys at the Roxy. It was no preparation for the giddy world she was joining. She was quick to realize this and sought expert help. Her antennae yet again twitched at the right time.

Rodgers introduced her to her Detroit days' idol – Diana Ross. She met Barbra Streisand. She was moving in the legend league. She wanted someone to guide her to that sort of status.

'Who's the best manager in the world?' she asked Rodgers and Jellybean Benitez. She did not wait for their answer. She thought it out herself. Who was the biggest pop star? Michael Jackson – go to the top of the class. No. Go to California and meet Jackson's manager, Freddy DeMann.

DeMann is always dapper, his moustache neatly trimmed and his hair slicked back. He no longer works with Jackson. He works with Madonna. She appeared in his Sunset Strip offices on a hot, smoggy day in July 1983, around the time her *Madonna* album was in the record stores. She was seriously blonde at the time. And determined. 'She had that special magic that very few stars have,' he remembers. DeMann was interested enough to fly to Manhattan to see Madonna do her stuff at Studio 54, then the hangout of choice for Bianca Jagger, the late fashion designer Halston, the Andy Warhol crowd and other up-market trendies. That crowd did not worry Madonna. DeMann was her concern. He had told her that he did not rate Prince so how would he rate her? And Michael Jackson, like Prince, was an exciting stage performer. Would DeMann like her? Would he manage her? Yes. And yes again. A formidable partnership was struck.

DeMann was taking care of business. Nile Rodgers, who had crafted Bowie's hit, *Let's Dance*, was in the recording studio with her. And so was Steve Bray the friend from the crazy days of the Blue Frogge in Detroit and the squabbling days in New York. The two were writing together again and four of their songs went on the *Like a Virgin* album.

The fireworks were about to go off. The title track of her second LP was also the first single, and the video was filmed in Italy, against the backdrop of the pillars and marble of Venice. It was almost the end of Madonna's career, and for the banshees of certain taste it is a pity that the lion did not eat her. The lion? Yes, the tame lion which co-starred with her. Just wasn't so tame, it seems. Madonna was to be performing confidently while the lion wandered over to her right side. She was not to be alarmed by it. She was provocatively leaning against a pillar – 'You make me feel,' hip push, 'like a virgin,' roll of the belly – when nudge, nudge, there's Leo the lion with his head between her legs. Right there! She says now that she was convinced he was going to take a bite out of her. She looked down from under her veil, looked away and then looked down again. Leo gave her the eye and then a deafening roar. 'Madonna Turns On King Of The Jungle Shock Horror' – how the newspapers would have loved that one.

Madonna was hot. The crucifixes, the bare midriff, the BOY TOY innuendo and her blatant sexuality also made her controversial. The 'Merry Widow' long-line bras were not uplifting to the Moral Majority. And there were millions of angry parents having to cope with youngsters who just wanted 'to be like Madonna'. Dr Sam Janus is an associate professor of psychiatry at New York Medical College and author of *The Death of Innocence*. His analysis: 'She was oblivious to the traditional standards of morality. The sexually explicit lyrics and her vulgar songs advocate prostitution.' Oh, well. What does Dr Danilo Ponce, a renowned professor of psychiatry at the University of Hawaii, have to say about that: 'The whole image Madonna projects is that of a tramp – of a streetwalker eager to sell her favours to the highest bidder.' Or her records? Dr Ponce went on: 'She flaunts her bare navel and dresses in lacy lingerie and black bras.'

What an advertisement. The legendary Frederick's of Hollywood, purveyors of all sorts of sexy underwear designed to give bottoms, busts and ardour a boost, recall the height of the *Like A Virgin* controversy. As well they should. Their sales were way up. Especially the black Merry Widows. In the first six months of 1985, there was a forty per cent increase says John Chapman, the company's merchandise manager. 'We knew her popularity was doing it. We were selling to a much younger element – girls were going for the innerwear-outwear effect.' Maidenform looked back at sales reports and found that their black push-up bra was a sell-out. Lily of France said their all-over lace body briefer did 'phenomenally' that year.

There were all sorts of ban-Madonna outcries. Margaret Scott, who is co-director of the United Parents Under God with head-quarters in Belmont, California, was active in that. Why?

'Our youngsters were being exploited and manipulated by Madonna. She took a public-be-damned attitude when it came to morals. Our kids were being victimized. The kids worshipped Madonna.'

They called her 'a porn queen at heart', 'a corrupting Pied Piper', 'a trashy tart', 'a slut'. The lady, they said, was a tramp. Madonna worried about that reaction for as long as it takes her to unhook her bra. Her attention was on the Wanna Be's, the fans who were buying her records and sending her to the top of the charts world-wide. In America, around 75,000 copies of *Like a Virgin* were dancing off the shelves daily. And the fans were desperate to see her live – she sold out three nights of concerts at Radio City Music Hall in New York in thirty-four minutes. The old record of fifty-five minutes belonged to Elvis Costello and Phil Collins.

The BOY TOY was no longer to be toyed with. She says it was all her humour, the mocking and mixing of sex and virginity, of crucifix and crotch. She says the fans tuned into her humour:

For so long people had been telling girls: 'You have to dress nondescript. You have to look masculine if you want to be in control.' And here was someone being very sexy and having fun and dressing up and doing exactly what these little girls wanted to do. And making all the decisions and having power and success. The people who adored me were the children who understood where I was coming from. The people who loathed me, didn't get it and my success pissed them off. There's a lot of idiots in the world. It makes for more interesting magazines. Wouldn't you rather read about a slut than a plain-Jane wallflower? I know I would. Anyway, I think it would be kind of boring if everyone just loved me 100 per cent.

But she would love it. A poll of half a dozen American psy-chiatrists showed she has an I-want-to-be-loved complex. And if you do not love her, or agree with her, or do what she wants, that

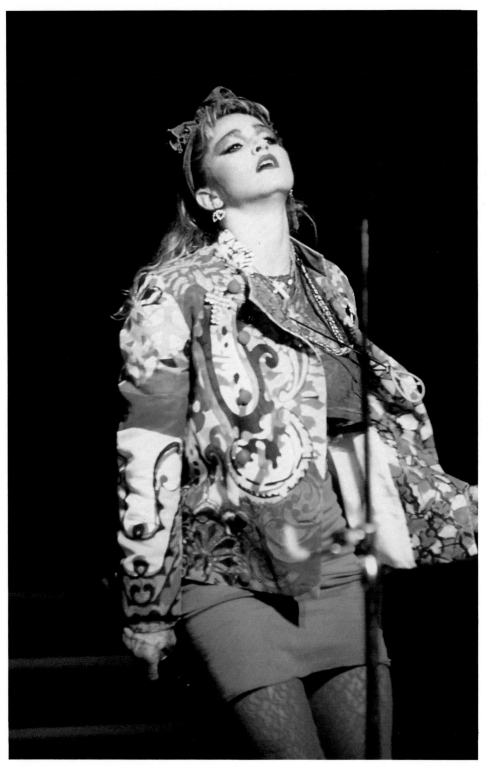

On stage during the Virgin Tour, 1985 *(Redferns)*

Opposite: A costume change for
Like A Virgin (LFI)

Above: Performing during the
Holiday period *(LFI)*

Left: With her band at Live Aid
(LFI)

Right: Playing a 1930's nightclub singer in *Bloodhounds of Broadway (Scope Features)*

Below: At the Tony Awards in New York, June 1988 *(LFI)*

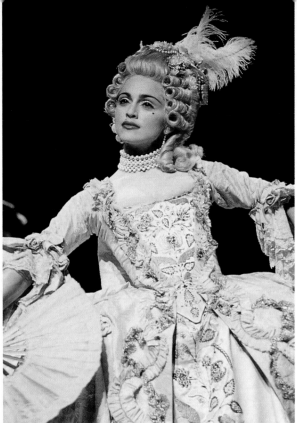

Above: Performing during the MTV Awards, 1990 *(LFI)*

Left: Singing *Sooner or Later,* from *Dick Tracy,* at the 1991 Academy Awards *(LFI)*

Above: With Jellybean Benitez during The Breakfast Club days in New York *(Scope Features)*

Left: With Sean Penn at an Amnesty Concert *(LFI)*

Above: With Sandra Bernhard at a benefit concert to save the rainforests, in New York 1990 *(LFI)*

is it. Be gone. That is her vulnerable spot. She has trouble with the other viewpoint, which is understandable when you are the most recognized star in the world. But it does not help in personal or business relationships. Her two years of living with Jellybean in a New York loft were almost over. He also wanted to be a star and was producing and recording on his own. There was no room in Madonna's world for two stars in the family as she was terrifyingly to discover.

Madonna's goals were endless. Her records were all over the pop charts. She had six at one time in the American Top Forty. She was working on her body, determined to be the healthiest and fittest star. She wanted to be a movie star. She had played a cameo role as a nightclub *chanteuse*, warbling two of her own songs in former Barbra Streisand lover, Jon Peters' film, *Visionquest*, (titled *Crazy for You* in the United Kingdom) and way inside her still wanted to be a movie star – a star: a big, major, massive, incredible, adored legend, like Marilyn Monroe.

SEVEN

THE MOVIES

'I can't conceive of living happily every after or happiness for a long period of time with one person. I change so much and my needs change also.'

MADONNA IN 1984

In the late summer days of 1984, Madonna spent a lot of time in her SoHo apartment in New York simply thinking, trying to clear her mind. She had climbed on to the rainbow. Now she wanted to ride it. As fast as possible. She knew she would have to go on tour. But she also wanted the movies. And she had heard about a picture that might just be her. In one of the most amazing – if somewhat lucky – marketing coups in show-business history, her desires dovetailed. It was as if someone had waved a wand and granted her every wish.

Also living in a SoHo loft was Susan Seidelman, who in 1984 was thirty-one, ambitious and the director of the cult film, *Smithereens*, which had been the surprise hit of the 1982 Cannes Film Festival. Seidelman sat on cushions to protect her spotless varnished floors while she read the script of a film entitled *Desperately Seeking Susan*. It was something of a New Wave fairy-tale with Susan disrupting the everyday and sex lives of all involved. The film relies on that elderly plot device, loss of memory. Temporary amnesia. It is a New Jersey housewife called Roberta who loses her memory and 'becomes' Susan. Mistaken identities and farce. Rosanna Arquette, who is like Audrey Hepburn masquerading as Sophia Loren – with her the gamin look she meets the full-figured woman – was offered and accepted the role of Roberta.

Susan was a small, $5 million budget film for Orion Pictures. To make it work, Seidelman needed a kooky, crazy, but believable actress in the title role. She heard on the New York grapevine – regarded as just ten minutes slower than the Hollywood buzz – that Madonna might be interested. Already 207 other actresses had shown their interest and been tested. Madonna did a screen test. Midge Sanford was one of the producers. Why did they pick Madonna over all the others? 'She had this presence you couldn't get rid of. No matter how good the other people were, we kept going back to her screen test.'

Seidelman was all for Madonna. Orion Pictures' executives had never heard of the singer. As Seidelman says, and hard as it is to believe now, Madonna was then 'just a pretty pop singer'. Ten months later, she would have been out of reach of such a small project. Then, she was prepared to work – and to learn. Her days of being the wise guy, the comedian in the school playground helped. So did the discipline from her dance training.

During the nine weeks of filming, we'd often get home at 11 p.m. or midnight and we'd have to be back on the set at 6 a.m. or 7 a.m. Half the time the driver would pick Madonna up at her health club. She'd get up at 4:30 a.m. to work out first.

Madonna admits to 'shitting bricks' when doing early scenes. But she was determined to learn. 'I think I surprised everybody by being so calm – I was gonna soak everything up.' She admits that there was something of a self-caricature about her Susan. But only so far.

At first it was hard to get producers to take me seriously because I was a rock star. I think they thought I would throw fits or do blow [cocaine] on the set or something. I think they were shocked when I showed up every morning like clockwork.

As Madonna's world and fame increased, so did the interest in the film. And Rosanna Arquette was disgruntled. A new song from Madonna, 'Into the Groove', was worked into the film. On a film location in the Pacific-Northwest, Arquette says:

The script changed when they got Madonna. I told them that if *Susan* was going to be a two-hour rock video, I didn't want to be part of it. A disco-dance movie wasn't what I signed on to do.

And American magazine had quoted her: 'I don't think I'd ever want to be as famous as Madonna.' She denied that to me saying:

I never said that. But I think it might be a bit of a prison for her to have that kind of fame. I mean, she can't go anywhere and that's a lot to lose. I'm an actor and I want to be able to do different things. I'm not a mega star – that's a tough thing to be.

Madonna went to work on *Desperately Seeking Susan* in November 1984, and at the same time *Like a Virgin* was released. By the New Year, the album and the single would be sitting at the top of the American record charts. And Madonna's life was about to change irretrievably.

There were the business things: the fantastic success of the Virgin Tour, which played to nearly 400,000 fans in twenty-seven cities with the Beastie Boys as the supporting band. On the last night of the tour, her father Silvio carried her off stage. The Material Girl was still Daddy's Girl. She renegotiated her record contract giving her much of the $8 million up front in a cash advance. She was not climbing the rainbow, she was sliding along it.

Personally, it was bumpy. Jellybean Benitez had sort of vanished with the New Year. 'We were still friends. I know a lot of her ex-boyfriends and I don't think she used them or me. She took advantage of opportunities given her. Other people do the same thing,' says Jellybean who, like most of her men, remains loyal. It was to get even bumpier that year. She was to meet and marry Sean Penn, be rumoured to be pregnant, have her naked body from the modelling days displayed all over *Penthouse* and *Playboy* magazines and go to court to try and stop the re-release of John Lewicki's soft-porn, *A Certain Sacrifice*. Her lawsuit argued that it was a poor quality film with an even poorer quality plot, never mind the orgies. Around that time, a ritzy apartment co-operative in New York's Central Park turned down her $1.8 million bid for a unit. Didn't want rock stars in the building. But Sean Penn wanted the Material Girl. Very badly. So badly that he played the romance without any of his trademark aggressive and impulsive style.

Madonna was still fixated by Marilyn Monroe. Wasn't she the original Material Girl? For the 'Material Girl' video, it was decided to reprise Monroe's best sequence from *Gentlemen Prefer Blondes*: Madonna would be Monroe. But she wanted really to get the feel of it. Bill Travilla, who designs for the ladies of the television series *Dallas* and *Knots Landing*, was responsible for Monroe's shocking-pink, cut-to-the-thigh gown in the 1953 film. He was surprised to see Madonna wearing it – or rather, a perfect replica of it – on her video. Travilla was not credited with the design but years later takes it in good humour, 'I felt, to paraphrase Madonna, like a virgin. I'd been knocked off for the very first time.'

The video was also the first time Sean Penn got up close to Madonna. It was a draughty recording studio in February of 1985. He, by no accident, turned up on the set of the video. He could hardly miss her fascination with Monroe. At this time, there was no evidence of Penn the hot head. They talked. They held hands. They did not date only each other and she said then:

I didn't feel swept off my feet, but he is somebody whose work I had admired for a long time. He's wild, though. He'll probably die young. We have so much in common. We were born one day apart [Penn was born 17 August 1960] and he and I have similar temperaments. I feel like he is my brother or something. . . . In fact, when I squint my eyes, he almost looks like my father when he was young. . . . He's really smart and he knows a lot. He's willing to play the outsider or nerd rather than the hero that everybody likes.

Madonna and Sean Penn, the Outsiders.

When they were first together on the West Coast, the doting Penn took Madonna on a forty-mile drive from his place in Malibu to Westwood, the university district of Los Angeles. To the back of the campus of the University of Los Angeles at California (UCLA) is Westwood Cemetery, the home of Marilyn Monroe's grave. She was shaking during the visit. The rose that is always there from baseball-great and ex-Monroe-husband, Joe DiMaggio, was on the grave. Later, Madonna said: 'He really loved her.'

And love, or something of an aberration of it, was to keep her going in the months ahead. No one – not even she or Sean Penn – knew what they were getting into. Madonna's early mentor Camille Barbone had something of an inkling when asked about that early relationship. She responded:

Madonna has always liked the rebel, the loner, in her men. James Dean is her idol. Sean Penn is not the first rebel in her life and probably won't be the last.

Penn has been around show business all his life. His father Leo is an actor turned television producer and director, and his mother is one-time Broadway star, Eileen Ryan. They dote on Sean and his five years' younger brother Chris, who were brought up in the surf-washed, sun-tanned community of Santa Monica. The family later paid three million dollars to move down the Pacific Coast Highway and into a Malibu hillside home.

Penn was a schoolboy when he began working in local Los Angeles theatre groups. At nineteen, he got a guest role on the long-running crime show, *Barnaby Jones*. He got more television work and then stage roles in New York. His big break was when he was cast opposite fellow Brat Pack member, Tim Hutton, in *Taps*. Then, he was a doped-out surfer in *Fast Times at Ridgemont High*, with Phoebe Cates in her pre-black suspenders and sexy television mini-series *Lace* days. It was a sign of the acting technique he was developing when he 'stayed in character' after the cameras stopped rolling. Director Amy Heckerling remembers he once 'lost' his character, but jumped right into being surfer Jeff Spicoli by stubbing out a cigarette in his palm. *Bad Boys* director Richard Rosenthal is a Penn fan. The film stamped Penn's screen image. He played a teen gangster and grew his hair to his shoulders, ignored the make-up department for a real tattoo (a wolf's head) and only gave in on having his teeth filed down when his mother objected.

'He likes to get into character. He's the most talented actor of his generation,' said Rosenthal who tells an amazing story:

We went out with some Chicago cops so Sean could get a 'feel' of it all. During the raid, some more cops arrived and thought we were criminals and told us to raise our hands. I complied, but for Sean it was a chance to see what it's like for a gang member to take on a cop.

He turned to the cop, who was the size of an apartment, and said, 'Fuck you'.

The cop picked up Sean and threw him into a wall. His nose was almost broken, but later he told me it was at that moment he finally became his character in the film.

Less charitably, *Bad Boys* co-star, Reni Santoni, recalls: 'I thought the kid had been watching too many Brando movies.'

Film executive Sherry Lansing, who produced *Racing with the Moon* which collapsed at the box-office – Penn refused to promote the film in which he co-starred with one-time lover, Elizabeth McGovern – still believes Penn has got to do something about himself. 'His career will be over if he doesn't change. He's talented but he's also self-destructive.'

But for all his supposed publicity shyness, Penn eats out at places like Sunset Strip's Spago which is always a swarm of cameramen. Once he walked out and into friend and Brat Pack 'godfather' Harry Dean Stanton. As flashbulbs popped, Penn zipped his jacket over his head and carried on the conversation with the bemused Stanton.

Penn liked proposing to actresses. First was Bruce Springsteen's sister, Pam. He met the sister of the Boss during filming

Ridgemont High. The wedding date was set for 20 February 1983. In April a year later, he was set to marry Elizabeth McGovern. Madonna intervened.

Even Penn's father Leo shakes his head when quizzed about his older son's appeal for the ladies: 'He has a big nose, small mouth and close-set eyes. He's moody and likes mischief.' And Penn himself tells a story which reflects just how far he is willing to go. It involves him and Brat-Packer son of Martin Sheen, Emilio Estevez:

One time me and my buddy Emilio planned this thing. It was one of those times when we sat around and said, 'We're really going to follow through on this. All the way. Nobody's gonna laugh.'

This guy Kelly always got off the school bus with Emilio. So one day I was around the corner with another buddy in my car. We had .22 calibre machine-guns with blanks. And Emilio had a blood squib – a big bag of fake blood. So he coaxed this guy Kelly into walking down to the ice-cream parlour with him.

We drive by – and open fire. Emilio does this great stuff. He squeezes the blood bag and it bursts all over his front. He hits the ground. Kelly has a skateboard in his hand, and he's freaking out. He starts to walk away in shock.

So we grab Kelly at gunpoint, put him in the back of the car, and we take off. He's so scared, he can't talk. We're wearing ski masks, and we're calling him Emilio as though we've got the wrong guy, right? We go up into the canyon. We stop and tell him to get out of the car, and we say, 'We're not going to hurt you, but we're gonna tie you to this tree and then we're gonna take off.'

This was our greatest, ever: out of the back of the car we take this gasoline can – it's full of water – and my buddy lights a match. The guy starts screaming. I pour the water on the guy, and my buddy flips the match at him.

Then we tell him. Emilio arrives, and we have a little picnic. And the guy has never been the same since.

No one who meets Sean Penn ever is.

He says his mother told him long ago about dealing with executives: 'She said when you go in don't picture them sitting behind a desk, but sitting on the toilet. It's amazing how that makes you strong.' As long as you don't get flushed away.

Penn was enjoying strong reviews for *The Falcon and the Snowman* when he first met Madonna. In the film, he and Tim Hutton starred as the title characters, two young and convicted spies. Penn sympathized with the 'Snowman' (he got the name for cocaine dealing), Andrew Lee Daulton, and still supports his efforts for parole. So much so that he forgot his shyness to appear on nation-wide television in the United States and say he would do what I can as things come up. During the research for the role it was more than 'you scratch my back, I'll scratch yours'. I think it became a friendship and out of this, within the bounds of what a friend can do, I will. Under different circumstances, I'd like to sit down and have a beer with him. Maybe sometime we'll do that.

But at a party for *The Falcon and the Snowman*, he spent two hours huddled behind a potted plant.

You get the feeling that it would be uncomfortable if Penn was cast as Hitler because his 'research' might involve starting a couple of wars. This deep research in changing mind and body is characteristic of DeNiro, but Penn insists in a rule-breaking talk-ative moment:

The one thing I don't like to see written about me is the whole DeNiro thing. I think it just doesn't matter. All that matters is what's on screen. I don't need to be thought of as a hard worker. I just want to be as good as I can.

'A lot of people will label him shy, but it's really just that he has a good sense of himself,' says Oscar winner, Tim Hutton, adding: 'He doesn't have to carry on or be an extrovert because he's got a real clear vision.' It is a vision clouded by Garboesque and violent acts; he appears to believe rocks are mightier than the Penn and shows a touch of the Red Indian about still camera – nervous, as though a camera click will kidnap his soul. One lady photographer at a 'publicity' function with Penn confided: 'He told me he had a water pistol and if I didn't leave he was going to fill the pistol with urine and squirt me.'

When Sean Penn and I met, he looked more in need of a Bloody Mary than a shot of pee. It was 8:30 a.m. on Hollywood's

Sunset Strip when they have hosed the streets and they seem to shimmer in the morning sun, clean after a night when they have been driven and prowled and mean. From three floors up in an art-deco hotel opposite the Comedy Store club Penn, who is not known for laughs, is watching the traffic start to move. He starts moving around the room. He has a powerful presence but looks more like a car hop with a hangover than a movie star. There is a lot of power in his right bicep as well as that tattoo of a wolf baring its fangs which he got for *Bad Boys*.

And *we're* doing Madonna jokes? A couple of years earlier that would have appeared an exercise in something close to self-destruction, a different sort of angle on Madonna's favourite knock-knock joke routine. But by then in 1988 Madonna and Sean Penn had been through marital mayhem, months of chaos with the world media simmering or roasting them depending on the flavour of the month or the news of the day. Tits and ass sell – Madonna would more than likely make page one of any lively newspaper at any excuse; the dead ones did not even know she was alive.

Sean Penn did, for every conscious moment of their relationship. But that Saturday morning he was as precise as he would ever be about the two of them. He used the word 'nigger' but carefully qualified that one had to understand how he was using 'this vulgar expression'. Go on.

I think the problems come about because I wasn't a good little nigger actor who remained quiet, made films and stayed out of the way of the Press.

Instead, I think I became labelled as the bad little nigger boy who married the white girl, a girl who was as white as they come. She belonged to them, to the public. And if anyone took her I think they thought it should be someone more acceptable like Donald Trump.

The public is very possessive about rock stars and about her in particular. They don't want to share her love.

Neither, of course, did he. Madonna and Sean Penn were hormones in a hurry; fantastic passion but then suspicious and later paranoid about their own and everyone else's motives.

But, in the beginning, everyone says it was true love. 'I'd never known Sean happier,' remembers his brother, Chris. Charlie Sheen told me: 'Sean's always been misunderstood. And probably most about how much he adores Madonna.' Sheen's brother, Emilio Estevez, voted the same way: 'I thought that was a lifetime partnership. I'd never write them off.' Their father Martin Sheen, the wise patriarch and honorary mayor of Malibu and misfits everywhere, said:

You just wanted it all to be perfect for them for they really were a well-suited couple. They both care and they both wanted to care for each other. I've often thought you can care too much and that spoils it.

Susan Seidelman, who was part of the Madonna crowd at the time, says:

She could have had anyone she wanted. If it was just for the sake of getting married, she could have married someone richer, better looking and more politically connected than Sean. I don't think she needed Sean in an opportunistic way. Movie people were already beating down her door.

For all the right reasons. She was becoming the hottest property in town. Any town. Anywhere. These were the Madonna-mania days, the beginning: 'Like a Virgin', 'Material Girl', 'Crazy for You', and 'The Gambler' from the soundtrack *Visionquest* were everywhere. And suddenly so was *Desperately Seeking Susan*. Orion Pictures, who had been reluctant to hire Madonna, now wanted to promote *her* film. It opened in nearly one thousand cinemas across America. It got a fair play from the critics. *Newsweek* magazine said of the title star: 'Not much subtlety is expected of Madonna or required – she has been typecast and fills the bill with delightful sluttishness.'

Ah, a slut again. But being well paid for it. Madonna saw the humour. The reviews were mostly kind and calling her 'a new star'. The clincher was that the film made money. And Hollywood, even if it had been ignoring Madonna's music, could relate to financial success, that particular bottom line was more important to them than her wiggling one was to the fans.

Madonna was hot. Hollywood was hot for her. From the Polo Lounge to Morton's, they were talking deals, packages and marketing. Herbert Ross, the veteran director who had made

Streisand's *Funny Girl* wanted her to star in the story of stripper, Blaze Starr (a project that would eventually get made with Paul Newman and newcomer, Lolita Davidovich), and Ray Stark, who is still one of the most powerful men in Hollywood, wanted her to be involved in a project about 1920s' torch-singer, Libby Holman. There was also talk of her starring for Disney in *Ruthless People* (Bette Midler got the role).

But Freddy DeMann proved why he was what Madonna herself knew she needed. He caught the moment. Madonna was talking deals all over Hollywood. She was hanging out with Penn and the Brat Pack and even by the Hard Rock Café at the Beverly Centre, which was more of a tourist than a trend trap. There were also the clubs like Helena's and its incongruous location diagonally opposite the tough Los Angeles Police Department's (LAPD) Rampart station where Robert Kennedy's assassin, Sirhan Sirhan, was held after the 1968 killing.

But she was also working out. Madonna was back living out of a suitcase. Her concert tour took her to comparatively small stadiums. DeMann knew what he had. The fans wanted to see Madonna. As close as they could get. He knew it from the Michael Jackson experience. DeMann grins: 'I wanted fans to be able to see her sweat.' They saw her sweat first in Seattle. At the same time her Wazoo line of clothing – lace tops, skin-tight leggings and midriff baring uplifting underwear – went on sale. Maripol, her friend and jewellery designer, who now has his own New York store remembers the days: '*All* the kids wanted to look like her. They were in the shop all the time. I called them the little Madonnas.'

And variations of them turned out in hordes for every concert. The Wanna Be's ('We wanna be like Madonna') could not have cared less when old fogey and Rolling Stone Mick Jagger said Madonna's songs were pinpointed by 'a certain dumbness'. Silly, would-be-pensioner, they thought. Madonna had been the hottest thing on Earth for at least three weeks so Mars bars to the Rolling Stones.

It was hard for Madonna, even with all the entourage help and protection, to run herd on this fame and acclaim. Her sister Paula said in a rare interview: 'Everyone needs someone to hold on to.' For Madonna, it was Sean Penn.

They found a tryst of a place in the Hollywood Hills. It was a white building, like a castle in one of those fifties' Hollywood epics when Errol Flynn was always the swashbuckling good guy and George Sanders or Basil Rathbone got skewered in the fading moment. For them it was romantic heaven. Was it haunted? For the practical of us, only be memories. The building had once belonged to legendary actor and boozer, John Barrymore. It was not a good omen.

EIGHT

ROMANTICS?

'I love being on stage and I love reaching out to people and I love the expressions in people's eyes and just the ecstasy and the thrill.'

MADONNA IN 1985

Madonna's rags-to-riches-in-rags story was catching on everywhere. Her popularity grew by every play of her videos on MTV and she was on again and again and again. John Sykes was MTV's programming vice-president as the Madonna phenomenon began: 'Madonna is a prime example of an artist who could use MTV to launch a career. We had no negative feedback. What video did was build up the expectations of her tour.'

She was preparing for the Like a Virgin Tour by building a work-out routine around a daily six-mile jog. Then, as today, she is almost totally vegetarian. She drinks Tab, chews sugarless bubble-gum and pigging-out for her is cheddar-cheese flavoured popcorn. The BOY TOY bad girl is always willing to be controversial but also wants to be cholesterol free. She is a long way from bourbon-swigging, drug-taking tragedies like Janis Joplin, Jimi Hendrix, and Jim Morrison. Madonna may not be clean-cut on stage but her energy is.

In the weeks before she and Penn became exclusively attached and moved into the former Barrymore home, there was much action in both their lives. She was on display. During her tour the 'Like a Virgin' number was designed to – and did – bring the house down. She strutted on stage in a silk wedding dress with a 24-foot long train. This particular virgin bride would then crawl between the legs of her musicians. Attention? She got plenty of it. And the fans loved the sub-teen sexual humour. Madonna walked on stage with a stereo-boom box and offered saucy jokes: 'Every lady has a box. My box is special because it makes music – but it has to be turned on.' Ouch! But her timing was spot on.

Youngsters were looking for an outrageous performer, someone they could 'adopt'. And could be like. For they could wear the shirts, T-shirts, a bracelet and cross-shaped earrings which were on sale at every concert; the marketing men were delighted because they were selling faster than anyone could remember, faster than fan paraphernalia at Michael Jackson or Prince concerts. You could see Madonna in concert, at the neighbourhood cinema, on 24-hour television and on posters in kids' bedrooms in much of the West.

Sean Penn was being moody down in America's Deep South where he was filming *At Close Range*. The film was being directed by his friend and later best man, James Foley. They got on well and it was Penn who persuaded Orion Pictures to give Foley the director's chair. His mother, Eileen Ryan, was appearing in the film and so was brother Chris. Christopher Walken was his co-star in the murder mystery based on a real-life, father-and-son crime syndicate.

Foley was one of the first to know how strong the relationship between Madonna and Penn was becoming. Others, mostly family members, soon found out. They were surprised. While Penn got stuck into the grind of making movies the lady in his life was rivalling Princess Diana for newspaper and magazine space. She was supposedly dating many men, including Don Johnson, who was then on his roll with *Miami Vice*. Dapper Don did not make the cut, although he tried. She is a fan of Billy Idol, but for his music and naughty sense of humour, not his body. There were persistent tales of heavyweight trysts with John F. Kennedy, Jr. which offered gorgeous copy about Madonna following through on her Marilyn fantasy with a Kennedy. Some say it is a fantasy she had not totally dismissed.

The truth was Madonna and Sean Penn were together every minute they could be. Although exhausted, she would call him every night after her performance and they would talk for half an hour. She wound down. Penn would often be winding himself up frustrated by his self-imposed chastity. He saw her perform in Miami and San Diego when he could get away from filming. And in Detroit, where he met her father and brothers and sisters. And found out to whom Madonna lost her virginity. Schoolfriend Carol Belanger remembers flipping through her High School Yearbook with Madonna and Penn. They stopped at a picture of Russell Long – the Cadillac Man. Belanger says she told Penn that Madonna 'broke a lot of hearts'. Penn was to turn around and do just that to the Madonna fans before the year was out. When the Virgin Tour arrived in Los Angeles, the Penn family and members of the Brat Pack were there. The long, hot summer was not far off.

James Foley says he was respectful of Madonna's relationship with Penn. Of the pre-marriage days: 'I'd known Sean for a long time and he'd never been happier.' Foley got lucky too. Madonna asked him to direct her new video of her singing 'Live to Tell' which was the closing song of *At Close Range*. He was glad to but says reflectively: 'Nobody knows what a major sweat those videos are.'

Diane Keaton is a close friend of Foley's – as is Cher and Barbra Streisand – and saw an early 'cut' of *At Close Range*. They became a constructive critical group and Foley says: 'Madonna is like Diane in that she has opinions and voices them without hesitation. Diane and Madonna have a lot of similarities and like and respect each other.'

Sean Penn does not like or respect the press, particularly the suede-shoe variety from the tabloids of Britain and America. Lots of people don't. It is just that he is rather more exuberant about it. In June 1985, the gossip factory was mass-producing stories that Madonna was pregnant. There had been hints that she and Penn were going to marry. Well, what other possible reason could there be for marriage? Love? Forget it – she's a BOY TOY and he's a WILD BOY. Some of that thinking was correct.

A writer and photographer from a British newspaper were sent to doorstep a motel on the outskirts of Nashville, Tennessee, and get happy snaps of the 'pregnant' Madonna who was visiting Penn on the *At Close Range* location. The lads got lucky or unlucky depending on how you view it. They had no idea if Madonna would be there. It was part of the old journalistic tradition of when-in-doubt-send. They had been sent.

When Penn saw them, his face went bright red with rage. He hammered and punched the writer, threw a rock at the photographer and then grabbed at his camera straps. Madonna was only a few steps away. She pulled a floral baseball cap over her eyes and ran back into the hotel. A very nasty incident which was not helped by the fact that photographer Laurence Cottrell had remained as cool as possible in the circumstances and kept his finger on the camera button. The photographs of the snarling Penn about to throw a rock went around the world.

The legend of the Poison Penns was building. And so was the talk of marriage. By now it was generally agreed they would marry – but when? And where?

The couple were hot. The new Burton and Taylor. They would star in a film entitled *Pipeline*, set in the Alaskan oilfields. They would do the comedy *Blind Date* (Kim Basinger and Bruce Willis finally made that one), and every other producer in Hollywood trying to pitch a package was talking Madonna and Penn.

On 13 August 1985, Madonna performed solo and with the Thompson Twins at Live Aid in Philadelphia. She was introduced by Bette Midler as 'a woman who pulled herself up by her bra straps and has been known to let them down occasionally'. Madonna had other thoughts as she strutted in Philadelphia. She and Penn were busy planning their marriage. Something old, something new, something borrowed, something blue? Try more military strategy. Penn was to greet his wedding guests with: 'Welcome to the remaking of *Apocalypse Now*.' He wasn't far off.

Madonna, who had boosted her career by being able to manipulate the public, was not such an artist when it came to privacy. She and Penn tried. The invitation, designed by Penn's brother Michael, read:

> *Please Come to Sean and Madonna's Birthday Party on*
> *the Sixteenth of August Nineteen Eighty Five. The*
> *Celebration Will Commence at Six O'Clock p.m. Please Be*
> *Prompt or You Will Miss Their Wedding Ceremony.*
> *The Need For Privacy and a Desire to Keep You*
> *Hanging Prevents the Los Angeles Location from Being*
> *Announced Until One Day Prior. RSVP by August 3 to:*
> *Clyde is Hungry Productions, 6521 Leland Way, Hollywood,*
> *CA 90028, (213) 460-6208. *Please include a phone*
> *number where you can be reached.*

Nuptials, Hollywood style. Don't call us – we'll call you. For all those guests hanging on for the wedding location, there was time to buy a wedding present. Madonna had gone the traditional route and registered with a store a list of gifts she would like. The Michigan girl, who had begun her career living out of rubbish bins in New York, was registered at Tiffany's and had selected two china patterns: Monet's Giverny which then sold for $260 a place setting and Coeur de Fleur from Tiffany's private stock which in 1985 was $660 a setting.

It was just an indication of just how far and fast Madonna had travelled. In shopping malls across America there were regular weekend Madonna lookalike contests. She had been photographed in Hawaii for a 'Madonna – 1986' calendar and

Barbra Streisand taped her video, 'Emotions', clutching a handful of photographs of Madonna. Hollywood was still at her door and the budget this time was $15 million for *Street Smart*, in which she was to appear with both Sting and Prince's protégé, Vanity, the three to star as a one-name rock trinity, in something that sounded very like *West Side Story*.

She was out jogging in Central Park in New York – not that healthy an activity given the high mugging rate – when she realized she could never again go anywhere public without a bodyguard. Concentrating on her running she at first did not realize that she had been recognized. When she did look over her shoulder, she was being pursued by about fifteen fans. She did not know they were just chasing autographs and panicked. She hurdled a fence and fell. She only scraped a knee, but she had lost control for a moment and swore that would never happen again.

Yet she had little control over the imminent remake, as Penn had put it, of *Apocalypse Now* on a bluff in Malibu. Penn's twenty-fifth birthday was on 16 August and Madonna was twenty-six the next day. It was quite a party for them both. Penn – although facing assault charges and a civil lawsuit for his bad-boy behaviour in Tennessee – seemed to have mellowed. He and Madonna had been playing house, renting the former Barrymore home for $1300 a month: they could see the HOLLYWOOD sign from the bedroom window. She recalls when he proposed:

I was jumping up and down on my bed performing one of my morning rituals and all of a sudden Sean gets this look in his eye and all of a sudden I knew what he was thinking. I said, whatever you are thinking I'll say yes to. That was his chance, so he popped it.

She says they celebrated by going out to a 7-Eleven convenience store and buying a bag of gob-stopper sweets known in America as 'jawbreakers'.

Not a traditional proposal or celebration, but wedding plans moved along in an orderly fashion from then. There was her wedding shower which was hosted by Nancy Huang, the girl-friend of Nile Rodgers. She had invited Madonna's friends to her Upper East Side apartment in Manhattan. Mariel Hemingway and Alannah Currie, from the Thompson Twins, were there. Oh, and six male friends of Madonna who dressed in drag by way of celebration. The gifts were lingerie, a push-button sequined phone and an assortment of jewellery. Madonna had bought herself, for $44,000, a midnight-blue Mercedes which was parked out in California where the celebrations continued a couple of days later in Hollywood with a 'bachelorette' party at the Tropicana. It is a tacky mud-wrestling club in a run-down area. Madonna went in a disguise of dark glasses, no make-up, her hair pulled back from her face and looked just like Madonna in dark glasses with no make up . . . she cheered as big-busted lady wrestlers flailed about in the mud.

Sean Penn was also getting ready for marriage – with a stag party. Madonna had the lady mud wrestler, but her husband-to-be was entertained by Kitten, who bounces off the measuring tape at 42-24-36. The party was in a private room above the Roxy nightclub on Hollywood's Sunset Strip. Penn's brother Chris, Tom Cruise, Robert Duvall, David Keith, Harry Dean Stanton and Cameron Crowe, who wrote *Fast Times at Ridgemont High*, were among the guests. The drinks were free. Kitten remembers: They were all pretty buzzed. Sean was feeling no pain. But he didn't fall on his face or anything. When he talked, he made sense. He's a very nice guy. He reminded me of a little boy, like he was eight years old and had got so many cookies he didn't know what to do with them.

Kitten Natividad did her strip routine with Penn slapping his knee in delight. Harry Dean Stanton arrived late and Kitten recalls: Sean picked up my blouse and said, 'See what you missed.' Then he shoved his face right into me. I didn't mind. Sometimes I do, but it was Sean's night and he could have done whatever he wanted. That was about as wild as it got.

No one really knows who leaked the location of the nuptials. But by the morning of the wedding, everyone knew it was in Malibu. By the afternoon the location was pinpointed. Television stations and newspapers rented helicopters and they did appear suddenly out of the sky like that famous scene in *Apocalypse Now*. I remember driving up Pacific Coast Highway from Santa Monica to Malibu to report the wedding for a British newspaper. It was mid-Friday afternoon and the weekend traffic heading north to Santa Barbara, Carmel and other retreats was already building up. The all-news radio was babbling the headlines and at the top of the news was The Wedding. Some commentator suggested it was the oddest coupling since Marilyn Monroe was turned on by the intellect of Arthur Miller, the couple who became known as the Hourglass and the Egghead. With a blazing red sun dipping down into the Pacific it seemed more beauty and the beast that day.

The world wanted sensation. They got media mania. And star paranoia. Who was out of order? The choppers buzzed the wedding of entertainment's most visible couple, the reigning king and queen of what seemed to be everyday's headlines. Crowds crushed around the estate. Madonna and Penn could have slipped off to Las Vegas and avoided such fuss. They didn't. They did it traditionally – with a Grand Prix of twists – on one of the most material pieces of real estate on earth. Malibu is where you flaunt rather than hide it. This is where you can lay on the sand and stare at the stars and vice versa. She forgot her outlaw black lace and wore an antique white gown, a low-cut number designed by Marlene Stewart, who costumed Madonna for her Virgin Tour. It was, recalls Ms Stewart, designed as 'a fairy-tale kind of thing with sort of a baroque feeling. We wanted a fifties feeling, something Grace Kelly might have worn.'

Well, we are talking rock royalty. The Queen of Pop added one of the twists to the traditional by giving the finger to a buzzing helicopter as her mother-in-law, Eileen Ryan, dabbed wedding-day tears from her eyes. The groom also stuck his head up the bride's dress. A new tradition? Maybe a Malibu one?

To set off her Cinderella gown, Madonna wore her hair in a French twist with a black bowler draped in cream-coloured tulle on top of it. What appeared like a beauty contestant's sash was draped across the dress, a silver and pink metallic neck covered in encrusted jewels. She walked down the white-ribboned aisle set out at the eight million dollar estate in shoes decorated in pearls and gold embroidery. Silvio Ciccone was at her side as the heli-copters buzzed like annoying flies in the clear blue sky above for the ten-minute ceremony in which the couple exchanged plain gold bands.

The groom wore a dark double-breasted, $695 off-the-rack Gianni Versace linen suit. The bride and groom are Roman Catholics and the Malibu clifftop where they took their vows had been blessed by a priest. White ribbons had fluttered on the bluffs all day like an open invitation to the helicopters that chattered all over them. White seats and benches, in sectioned, serried ranks and enough to accommodate 200 guests, had been laid out two hours before the ceremony at the lavish home of film producer Kurt Unger. Unger, a neighbour of America's major talk-show host, Johnny Carson, is a close friend of Penn's parents. The massive catering tent was Pepsodent-white like the bunting and ribbons covering the tennis courts. White lily pads floated in the swimming pool. But there was anger among the guests over the helicopters which delayed the ceremony. Producer James Day who was there as a guest says: 'Guests were hoping Sylvester Stallone would turn up and do a Rambo on the 'copters.' He did not. Many others did. And they went through what seemed like presidential security.

Tom Cruise, David Keith, Andy Warhol, Christopher Walken, Martin Sheen, Diane Keaton and Carrie Fisher were all formally dressed. Cher set off her not-so-traditional outfit with a spiky purple punk hair-do. 'I thought this was a secret,' complained actress Rosanne Arquette as she, along with other famous faces, submitted to being frisked by security men in smart slacks and blue jackets which hid their two-way radios. Penn had also arranged for guards with infra-red binoculars to 'frisk' the perimeters of Unger's estate. An Italian photographer wearing camouflage gear and a blackened face, for all the world looking like an SAS man, had been caught and ejected from his hunter's hide in the shrubbery just before the 6:30 p.m. ceremony.

Judge John Merrick, who conducted the bizarre event, recalls that despite the choppers he thought it was 'dignified'. 'I was shouting but she was answering as loud as she could. I think she enjoyed it all.'

Best man, James Foley, smiled through two weeks' growth of beard for most of the ceremony, and Madonna's sister Paula, who was her matron of honour, helped pacify the bride and groom as the choppers continued to hover overhead. They told them to forget about the intrusion and concern themselves with their own lives – and it was with a brave face that Madonna turned to her father before taking her vows and said: 'Bye, Dad.' The music was 'Moments Of Love', but as the music was drowned out by the helicopters, Penn's face got redder and redder.

'The ceremony was lovely. Madonna was lovely, but I couldn't hear a thing – nobody could,' recalls *Deer-Hunter* Oscar winner, Christopher Walken. As the official ceremony ended, the *Chariots of Fire* theme started up. Penn lifted the veil pinned to Madonna's black bowler hat and gave her a lingering kiss. Then, hand in hand, they clambered up to the balcony, and grinning, began waving to their guests. Madonna leaned backwards to the crowd before hurling her bouquet of white roses into the sky. It was aimed towards a group of her single girlfriends. 'Catch it, catch it,' she yelled at them. The Bad Boy and the Boy Toy were wed as Penn toasted, 'The most beautiful girl in the world'.

Service was quick for the 200 guests after the ceremony. Malcolm McClaren's *Madame Butterfly* blasted from loudspeakers as waiters scattered around pouring $100 bottles of Cristal champagne. A feast was served by the chefs from Spago: a five-tier hazelnut cake with sugar flowers; lobster ravioli; rack of lamb; swordfish; and baked potatoes stuffed with sour cream and caviar. Wines included California's Acacia Pinot Noir. There were three fully stocked, 8-foot long bars.

Cher remembers a wonderful moment. When it came to cutting the cake, Madonna turned to her friend saying: 'Hey, you've done this before. Do you just cut one piece or do you have to slice up the whole thing?'

Outside, the press were still gathered. One man armed with a two-way radio was trying to talk to his airborne colleague: 'Mad dog to mad dog one ... do you copy?' Inside the guests were gasping at the wedding presents which had a room of their own. There was a 1912 antique silver-tea service from British producer John Daly, who was responsible for *The Falcon and the Snowman*. An antique jukebox with two dozen of Madonna's favourite oldies – half of them Motown numbers – from Michael Ostin, an executive of Warner Brothers Records. And there were several sets of Tiffany china. Disc jockey Terence Toy had got the dancing going with some Big Band Swing numbers but by 8 p.m. was beginning to liven things up. He blasted out Motown's dance numbers and then Madonna's own 'Into the Groove'.

Which was what the couple planned to do on their four-day honeymoon at the Highlands Inn in Carmel, the seaside community quietly settled between Los Angeles and San Francisco and known around the world because of the two-year tenure of Mayor Clint Eastwood. For $225 a night, the Highlands Inn offers peace, quiet and privacy which Penn and Madonna needed. One room-service waiter tells of the day he delivered to their suite: 'I couldn't believe by eyes. They were both sitting in the bath together – and they had their clothes on. And the bath was full of water. They were not embarrassed about it, but I was.'

The couple were in room 429 and registered as M. Ochs. It was an in-joke on the play of 'Madonna Ochs'. The late Phil Ochs was a sixties protest folk-singer who was overshadowed by Bob Dylan. He became a disillusioned, forgotten, and extremely difficult character: 'Phil was an asshole long before it became fashionable,' said Penn, who liked the idea. He had driven them north in his black Mercedes. Madonna was wearing a black sweatsuit. 'She wore the same sweatsuit for three days,' recalls a maid who revealed: 'They brought their own beer cans with them. They gave me one and we all held hands while we had a drink.'

Madonna appeared to survive on room-service strawberries and cream, and supplies of champagne, orange juice and popcorn from the hotel's food shop. One night, they went out to dinner at the Hog's Breath Inn which is owned by Clint Eastwood. It is a favourite eating pub for Carmel locals, but also popular with tourists. By going there – and why they did? – any belief that their whereabouts could be secret was gone. By morning, the fans, the press and the pararazzi were heading for Carmel. The honeymoon was over.

Reality and the business of finding a family home took its place. They had been looking for a long time. Penn favoured something in Malibu with a good number of acres. One of his Pack remembers asking him if he planned to fence off any property he might get and was told by an unsmiling Penn: 'A fence, nothing. We're going to have gun towers.' Madonna had not seen any gun towers in Beverly Hills or Bel Air where she had been looking. Her search almost led to an embarrassing run-in with another material girl, Nancy Reagan. Playwright Neil Simon had put his lavish Bel-Air home up for sale. First Lady Nancy was interested but dithering. She looked around twice. Then she brought friends over. Then she arrived at separate times with three different sets of decorators. The Simon asking price was $3.5 million. All of this was unknown to Madonna who was being shown property by a Beverly Hills real-estate agent. She fell for Simon's property instantly and offered a bid closer to the asking price. Simon was stuck. He pleaded a change of circumstance and took the house off the market.

Madonna and Penn were headed for a $3.5 million estate, shielded by the mountains that used to be roamed by the Chumash Indians. They created more barriers with a high, electrified wall fence. Penn wanted more security. Steel spikes were ordered and placed along the top of the walls. It was a sort of marital Fort Knox. Despite that, it was the scene of some of Madonna's happiest moments. And her most terrifying.

But for the moment, they were lovers scouting shops in Los Angeles and New York for furniture, for bric-à-brac for their home. By October there were already rumours that the marriage was in a desperate way.

NINE

ANOTHER DAY, ANOTHER BRAWL

'*H is temperament is similar to mine.*

That doesn't always make for an ideal relationship,

but I don't know what will happen.'

MADONNA IN 1985

It was only a few weeks after the wedding that Madonna sought psychiatric help. Her friends urged her also to persuade Penn into seeking professional help. When Penn had turned extraordinarily violent, into a wild-eyed madman during his attack on the two British journalists in Nashville, she had been speechless. 'Throughout the whole thing she never said a word to either of us,' recalls Laurence Cottrell, the photographer at the scene, adding: 'She just stood there and watched us as he did his thing with the rock.'

Now it seemed like another day, another brawl. Seven weeks after the wedding, Penn was spitting and swearing at photographers outside Wolfgang Puck's West Side celebrity hangout 'Chinois' in Santa Monica. Madonna was covered up with a coat

---

and laughing: 'Where are we? I can't see where I'm going.' Penn did not find any of it funny.

A Certain Sacrifice with a brunette Madonna went on sale in video stores in October 1985, just as Madonna and Penn were driving, running, or hiding from photographers in Los Angeles and Manhattan. Penn went to Nashville to face his assault charges. He was fined $100 and given a ninety-day suspended sentence.

Madonna and matrimony seemed to be bringing out all the acrimony in Penn. Around the celebrity crowd hangouts in New York and Los Angeles, they were known as 'S and M'. They were also one of the best-known couples in the world. Madonna had convinced herself that acting was what she wanted more than anything. But she was still deeply in love with Penn and determined, as a good Catholic girl should be, to keep the marriage intact. She also had much respect for Penn as an actor, as a mentor.

This was the start of another obsession for her – to win the title role of *Evita*. She had met quietly with producer Robert Stigwood and Penn was unaware how keen she was on the role. With him, she was talking a joint project. But then, as now, Madonna wanted movie stardom on the Marilyn Monroe scale. She saw *Evita* as the vehicle to provide that. Seymour Stein, who had launched her career recalls:

I knew from the moment she walked into my hospital room that she would be a star. She had the kind of self-assuredness that convinced me she was a very determined lady. I don't know about ruthless. When men are ambitious they're called ambitious; when women are ambitious they're called ruthless. There's no ego problem there. She's in a hurry. She's very, very serious about what she does.

She knows what she wants. Her talent has been obscured because of the fuss about everything else. But nobody tells her what to do.

It also seemed that way to Hollywood producer Julia Phillips, who had been involved in major box-office successes like *The Sting* and *Close Encounters of the Third Kind* before she dived into an abyss of drugs. When Phillips had a meeting with Freddy DeMann at

Morton's restaurant in Hollywood, she was won over by him. 'He was managing Madonna, the hottest female to come along since Barbra Streisand.' In her controversial book *You'll Never Eat Lunch In This Town Again* which chops up many Hollywood notables, she writes about 'taking a meeting' with Madonna and Sean Penn whom she calls the Prince and Princess. She says her martini arrived at the same time as the couple.

I am torn for a moment between saying hello, changing seats, and taking a long sip. I do all three without embarrassing myself. She is dyed platinum and dressed from head to toe in black leather. He is in jeans and leather jacket, what a surprise. He is a dim bulb in her supernova aura. She has the same amazing pale perfect skin that Barbra Streisand has. I have always imagined that Marilyn Monroe's skin was like that too. It is impossible not to think of Marilyn Monroe when you see Madonna even if you know that that's because she has designed herself so that you will think that way.

Phillips asks if they want drinks. Madonna orders a Perrier water. Penn looks at Phillips' martini and starts to order a beer. Madonna squeezes his knee and he changes his mind. The film discussions really do not go anywhere concrete. But Phillips and DeMann continued to talk, to meet. She was pushing a female version of *Carnal Knowledge*, the 1971 film which starred Jack Nicholson as a sexual adventurer. In Phillips' working of the film, Madonna would play the sexual experimenter. Madonna was taken by the thought of the memorable Nicholson role and in turn gave DeMann permission to pursue the idea with Warner Brothers. But there were complications because of a similar project.

Still, every studio in town wanted Madonna in *something*. In *anything*. And they were miffed when Handmade Films, in Hollywood termed an upstart company, run by former Beatle George Harrison, won her services. Handmade had made *The Life Of Brian* and *A Private Function* and now had Madonna starring in the $15 million *Shanghai Surprise*. The hook had been her co-star, Sean Penn, who would play a down-at-the-heel adventurer to Madonna's missionary in 1930s China. They were getting $1 million each. As well as some surprising perks.

The couple would have total script approval, which was a nerve considering Madonna's lack of film experience. And they would have a double bed with Japanese screens in their dressing room. Their involvement in publicity for the film could be 'requested' not 'demanded'.

Publicity? They got more than they ever dreamed.

Macao has been a magical movie name since the RKO Studio days when Robert Mitchum wooed Jane Russell and chased William Bendix. A city of intrigue, gambling and mystery, the Portuguese settled here in 1557. Relations between them and their one billion neighbours next door in China have always been reasonable – a reasonable people who were about to encounter a rather unreasonable young man. Penn was becoming more and more insecure by the day. His wife was the entertainment world's hottest new talent and he was increasingly being regarded as difficult and excess baggage. Was he worth the trouble?

The *Shanghai Surprise* film company set themselves up in the Oriental Hotel, a tower block of East meets West accommodations with wonderful service. The couple were assigned two bodyguards trained in martial arts. Security men would seal off the swimming pool when Madonna wanted a paddle. They put on disguises to go out to restaurants. It was Leonel Borrahlho's job to see through the disguises.

He was sixty-one when the Penns arrived in Macao and the correspondent on the island for the *Hong Kong Standard*. Mr Borrahlho, who is now retired and living in Macao, was a member of the *Leal Senada* – the Loyal Senate – and a man of propriety and dedication. He was asked to get photographs of this famous Hollywood couple. While others doorstepped the lobby of the Oriental Hotel, the enterprising Mr Borrahlho found out which floor the Penns were staying on. He then found himself a hiding place on the eighteenth floor near their suite. Late one afternoon he got lucky and unlucky at the same time. He was in position as

Madonna and Penn and their bodyguards emerged from the elevator. From behind the door of a 'blind waiter' he and his camera popped.

Penn panicked. 'Who let you in? What are you doing here? Can't you see my wife's trembling?' Mr Borrahlho says he saw Penn's fist coming towards him but it was stopped short by one of the bodyguards. The noise, the scuffling, left everyone seeing events differently. A bodyguard tried to grab the camera which was hung around the photographer's neck. Mr Borrahlho remembers karate chops and kicks as his camera strap held and his neck was injured in the tug-of-war.

'I was only doing my job. I didn't expect this kind of "Ugly American" behaviour,' says Mr Borrahlho. Seemingly, Penn's reputation for never meeting a photographer he could not wait to punch had not got that far East. Now it had arrived with force and Penn was to be called uglier things over the next few days as all manner of legal wrangling went on. Leonel Borrahlho used his platform of the *Hong Kong Standard* and his political clout in Macao to make things as difficult as possible for the film-makers, and particularly Penn.

Madonna was angry and frustrated by the Penn-inflicted circumstances. She had liked the script for the film which was based on Tony Kendrick's novel, *Faraday's Flowers*, and saw it as a chance to create something like *The African Queen*, with she and Penn as today's Bogart and Hepburn. She enjoyed the feel of the era and the dressing up as Gloria in the period clothes. She turned herself into a Jean Harlow-style platinum blonde as Gloria, a woman who runs away from the Depression in America to seek fulfilment in the Orient. Madonna wanted to be fulfilled as an actress. She wanted to prove she could act. Gloria, she felt, was a woman so different to her that she would have to give an Oscar-worthy performance to pull the character off. Gloria, unlike her she thought, was not in touch with her emotions. But both she and her character had to contend with Penn.

As did George Harrison and his Handmade Films. Chris Nixon was the publicity man on the film. It was a thankless job.

But Nixon knew his job and how to turn the nasty fracas and publicity around: give the reporters and photographers something about which to write and point their cameras. Penn thought the suggestion preposterous. The Prince and the Princess were not posing. Or talking. Nixon, who in hindsight was proved correct, suggested that the film needed every help it could get. He was sacked. His comment? 'Penn is a very aggressive, arrogant little shit.'

In several corners of the world, Nixon would be hard put to find an argument about that remark: especially on the set of *Shanghai Surprise*.

But Madonna was still standing by her man, while at the same time reading everything she could about *Evita*, which was about the only distraction she could enjoy. She was in the Oriental Hotel sauna when a girl reporter cornered her and asked if she was enjoying herself in the Orient. 'What? Being harassed? No. We didn't think we'd have any problems here.' She was also asked about the Borrahlho incident: 'That guy acted like a real jerk.' But, despite the bravado, Madonna worried. This was not how it was supposed to be. It certainly was not looking like *The African Queen*.

George Harrison flew to Hong Kong to referee an increasingly difficult situation. Madonna saw it as a test. There were big black rats under her trailer. The two-legged kind were on the streets and these Chinese gangsters began making extortion demands. Extra security men were brought in because of a death threat made against Madonna, according to a source who worked on the film. Madonna was depressed. This was only her second film. The go-for-it-I-can-do-it young girl who had conquered New York was feeling totally insecure and inadequate in a foreign land.

Penn, as Mr Wade, a grifter on the loose in the Orient, seemed to be staying in character around the clock. Director Jim Gorrard, then fifty, had earned his spurs on television mini-series and had been strongly recommended to Penn by Martin Sheen. But Madonna had seen her young husband challenge Gorrard's decisions and that ruled him out as a shoulder to cry on. And neither was Harrison, the quiet Beatle, whom Madonna regarded as a rather sweet but hapless character. There was no father figure for her anywhere in the Orient. Under all this emotional stress, she clung on to Penn. It was them against the world and she had never before nor would ever again get on so well with her husband.

For her, Harrison was an old-timer, someone from the past. She had displayed such youthful arrogance before. Just before leaving New York to begin filming *Shanghai Surprise* she and Penn had been invited by Yoko Ono to a private dinner party in honour of Bob Dylan. Wandering through Ono's Dakota Building apartment, she went into the kitchen where Dylan and David Bowie were talking. When she returned to the living area, where there was a crowd chatting over drinks and nibbles, she could not stop herself blurting out: 'Thank God there's somebody here to talk to – there are only old folks in the kitchen.'

She was about to discover how hot the 'kitchen' can get as she flew off to England to continue filming.

At Heathrow Airport the press waited for her arrival. Penn was to join her later at Shepperton Studios in Middlesex and on location at a former sanatorium near Virginia Water in Surrey. The madness began long before Madonna got anywhere near the lunatic asylum. Libby Krall, 5 ft. 10 in. tall and a 'minder' to Tina Turner, Tatum O'Neal, Goldie Hawn and Liza Minnelli and the first female security officer at the Xenon night-club in London's Piccadilly, had been asked to take on Madonna's protection on the basis that she could guard her even in the toilet. 'I said thanks, but no thanks,' remembers Libby, explaining: 'I just didn't want the hassle.' But there were enough enthusiastic male bodyguards around Heathrow. They had been told to get Madonna out of the airport quickly. No pictures. No press. And playing Garbo was, of course, the only way to ensure a rumpus. Madonna's Mercedes sent one photographer flying. 'Maimed By Madonna' shouted a headline.

The war of the press against the Poison Penns began and had a good run at the beginning of March 1986 because it was all quiet on other Western fronts. Bodyguards with dogs patrolled outside the sanatorium. And no one seemed to know where the film was going. Because of the problems in Macao and Hong Kong, several action sequences had not been filmed. Madonna and Penn thought they were making a love story. The producers were looking for a *Raiders Of The Lost Ark*. Both were to be terribly disappointed.

Madonna told Harrison that she felt she was working through the Third World War. He called a press conference at the Kensington Roof Gardens. For him, the scenes were a reminder of being mobbed in his Beatle days: 'In the sixties, all people could do was knock the Beatles so I've been through it all myself.' But Harrison admits he was astonished at the pandemonium Madonna's press conference started. He feared for their safety. Police were called to escort Madonna away. There had been one notable quote from her: 'I have nothing to apologise for.' At that time, she had not seen *Shanghai Surprise*. And not many people ever did.

Penn hated the film and told his friends never to see it. Madonna regarded it as a miserable experience but bounced back as she always does on the optimistic side. She had no regrets. She had learned from it. And mostly what she had learned was to take and keep control. Of the work in progress. Of the press. What had begun as a game of titillating and teasing the media, now was a serious part of the business. It knocked out her plan to co-star in *Blind Date*. She had been told she would have approval of her leading man. Bruce Willis, who was hot from *Moonlighting*, had already been cast. That took control away from Madonna – she was out of the project. And into making her third LP, *True Blue*. She dedicated it to Penn whom she called 'the coolest guy in the universe'.

The inside word was that Madonna was on the way out. She had had her run as a slut rock queen, as the BOY TOY, the Pied Piper of porn as some would have it. Then, the critics began hearing *True Blue*. Almost all the reviews talked of the control and character in her singing. She co-produced the album with Steve Bray and friend and record producer, Patrick Leonard, and with them wrote the songs. She also made a few lyrical changes to a song written by professional songwriter, Brian Elliot, called 'Papa Don't Preach'.

The first single from *True Blue* was 'Live to Tell' from Penn's and James Foley's film, *At Close Range*. It would be a world-wide number-one hit and make much more impact than the movie. It was then she easily declined the invitation of Don Johnson, then the hottest thing on TV, to sing on his new album, and instead 'Papa Don't Preach' was released to record-chart success and an almighty controversy.

Robert Hilburn, the pop-music critic of the *Los Angeles Times* and one of the most highly regarded in America, had watched the Madonna backlash build up in the music world. He says *True Blue* proved that those betting against Madonna's longevity were going to lose.

All along she had shown hints of ambition and sharp show-business instincts that suggested she was a survivor. Some people will never take Madonna seriously just as many never took Marilyn Monroe seriously. Novelty images – especially that of the sex symbol – are hard to erase. But talent far outshines novelty. Like David Bowie, she *visualises* music.

And 'Papa Don't Preach' could have been created for MTV. It tells the story of an unwed girl who decides to keep her baby but wants her father's approval for doing so.

> *Papa don't preach, I'm in trouble deep*
> *Papa don't preach, I've been losing sleep*
> *But I made up my mind, I'm keeping my baby*
> *I'm gonna keep my baby, mmm . . .*

Madonna delivered the song in a passionate, immediate almost sob. It started trouble. Alfred Moran of America's Planned Parenthood said:

The message is that getting pregnant is cool and having a baby is the right thing and the good thing and don't listen to your parents, school, anybody who tells you otherwise – don't preach to me, daddy. The reality is, what Madonna was suggesting to teenagers was a path to permanent poverty.

Everybody I've talked to believes she has had more impact on young teenagers than any other single entertainer since the Beatles.

The pro-lifers backed Madonna. First Parents Resources Centre founder, Tipper Gore, endorsed the song as it told of a woman deciding against an abortion. Feminist lawyer, Gloria Allred, and the National Organization of Women demanded that Madonna speak out supporting their pro-abortion view.

Madonna tried to steer away from such an emotive issue. She thought the song was about a celebration of life. Her video – with the fine actor Danny Aiello as her father – features Madonna as a shivering waif waiting for her father's answer. Waiting for daddy's approval. Aiello calls her a 'true superstar' and recalls being so impressed by her that he told her: 'Madonna, I look into your eyes and I can see your heart.' He says she told him: 'I'm not that soft.'

The song could have been written for her. It wasn't. Brian Elliot was responsible for this landmark in Madonna's career. Elliot is a bearded jolly forty-year-old, with a studio-office close to North Hollywood High School.

My studio window is the biggest mirror in North Hollywood – girls stop to look at their reflection, fix their hair, talk things over. Their gossip is unbelievable. I developed an empathy for the things they got themselves into. The girl in the song is a composite. It's a reflection of things overheard. I wrote it for another singer, but someone at Warner Brothers heard it and thought it would be perfect for Madonna. If someone else had sung it, then it would have had an entirely different resonance. But Madonna is larger than life. I didn't think of the social consequences. I knew it was freighted with all kinds of reality. But basically I wanted to write a good piece drama, something that would fit into *West Side Story*. Picture that song sung by someone waif-like and it becomes something entirely different.

It's more of a plea for compassion from the father not a 'Hey, I'm going to keep my baby whether you like it or not'. I thought it was very strange casting, matching the song with Madonna, but it worked.

TEN

JAILHOUSE BLUES

'I have my insecure moments and that puts a lot of strain on people. You take things out on the person you love and that causes fights, alienation, grief, shrink sessions, and a lot of ca-ca.'

MADONNA IN 1987

Ironically, in the months leading up to the 'Papa Don't Preach' debate, the gossip mill was insisting that Madonna was pregnant. But then there was the incident which started the real decline of Madonna's marriage.

It happened in Helena's night-club where Penn, like Jack Nicholson and Anjelica Huston, had become a 'regular'. So was musician and songwriter David Wolinski, who was sitting with a group of record executives a little after midnight. 'Hawk' Wolinski, who had worked with Madonna and played drums for Chaka Khan, was chatting away. Farrah Fawcett and Ryan O'Neal were at the bar. So was Drew Barrymore from *E.T.* and Harry Dean Stanton, Robert Duvall and singer Glen Frey. They all saw Wolinski go down after a sucker punch. Penn and Madonna were leaving the club when Wolinski, who was sitting with a party of mutual friends, saw her.

The official police report on the case, released here for the first time, gives the most dramatic account of the inexplicable madness of the moment. And the worrying violence. File 86-0217877 from the Rampart Police Station dated 12 April 1986, and timed 00.30 hours reads:

Victim stated at the above date and time victim was seated at a table when the singer and friend Madonna walked by. Victim stated to Madonna, 'Good night'. The suspect, Madonna's husband, stated: 'Why did you try to kiss my wife?'

Suspect then appeared to go mad and with his right fist struck victim on the left side of the face. The victim fell off chair and was on the ground. Suspect picked up a chair and started hitting victim with the chair and kicking victim while on the ground. Suspect then picked up a podium and was about to throw it on victim however was stopped by unknown citizen. Suspect then departed the location along with wife Madonna.

The next line reads:

Injuries: Victim has bruises and swelling on left side of face. Victim further has large bruises on legs and lower body. Victim will seek meeting with his own doctor.

A follow-up report reads:

Investigating officer spoke to the victim who stated that he was attending a private party at a club known as Helena's. The suspect's wife came to the victim's table and spoke to several members of his party as well as the victim. The victim was then approached from the rear by the suspect who accused the victim of bothering his wife and struck the victim several times with his closed fist. The victim fell to the floor and in a semi-conscious condition. He was then kicked several times by the suspect. The suspect walked over to the entry section of the club and picked up a small podium. He then ran toward the victim and attempted to strike him in the head. The suspect was stopped by several patrons. He was then forcibly removed from the premises.

Contacted Michael Ostin who was present during the fight. Mr Ostin stated that he saw the suspect kick and hit the victim. Mr Ostin further indicated that the victim did not fight back as he appeared dazed from the first blow.

The report reveals more than details about the incident. It shows the attitude of those around Madonna and Penn. The Michael Ostin in the police report was none other than the executive of Warner Brothers Records' creative department and the very man who had lined up Madonna with Brian Elliot's 'Papa Don't Preach'. But rather than protect Penn by saying little, he told the investigating officers that not only did Wolinski not start the brawl, but that also he was knocked out of any proper contest by Penn's surprise first blow.

That night, Madonna had seen a colleague and friend hurt by Penn for no reason and another colleague indicate the blame without any hestitation. She talked to her psychiatrist about it all the next day. In the meantime, other witnesses said Wolinski did not start the fight. The matter-of-fact police blotter report of the incident gives the immediacy of the incident. It does not reflect the cold fury all those at Helena's that night saw in Penn.

Madonna always knew just how far it could have gone that night and suffered nightmares because of it. Some of her closest friends found Penn spoiled and immature. And they were scared by his temper tantrums – one of which she had just seen in full, bloody close-up.

'She seemed to be having a great time at Helena's. She was real bubbly and smiling a lot,' says one of the Warner Brothers' party. Madonna still records for the company so they are careful, but he added: 'When Penn pulled that ambush punch, her mood changed just like that.' Ryan O'Neal rushed over from the bar and tried to help Wolinski.

'The marriage had been undergoing stress all the time,' says an actor friend of Madonna's who called the Wolinski incident 'the first real traumatic episode for her'. He explained: 'Wolinski was someone she knew and it really shook her up.'

Despite being disturbed and shaken, Madonna contacted Wolinski and after apologizing for the attack asked him not to press charges. Wolinski said that an apology from Penn would be more in order. There was talk of an out-of-court settlement, but in the event the Los Angeles City Attorney went ahead and prosecuted Penn. Behind the scenes in the City Attorney's Office the mood was that Penn, be he Mr Madonna or not, needed to be brought into line. Later, he would be fined $1700 and put on a year's probation which was not exactly the Botany Bay treatment that the prosecutors had been talking about.

However, Madonna was relieved. Penn had not been showing great restraint before his court hearing. They had bought an $850,000 Manhattan apartment on Central Park West earlier that year. That was the location for more run-ins with photographers. For Penn, the brawl never seemed to be over.

Madonna detests failure and that made her work even harder at her marriage. The thought of all the carrion told-you-so's around the world picking over her divorce made her cringe. But it did not stop her from taking precautions. The Central Park West apartment was in her name only. As were the various companies she was setting up to develop projects – particularly films – for her. She still had not lost sight of *Evita*, but James Foley brought her a film initially called *Slammer*, which was never to have the impact that title implied. It became *Who's That Girl?*, a dizzy-dame movie with Madonna as a wrongly jailed ex-convict who is released to find revenge and fun. Her Nikki Finn takes Griffin Dunne's straight-arrow lawyer, Loudon Trott, along for the ride. It is quite a long one and Madonna's voice grated. The critics snarled. Madonna had seen it as her Judy Holiday turn. Or a homage to Cary Grant and Katharine Hepburn's *Bringing Up Baby* – during filming, a wild cat, a cougar not Madonna, got loose on the streets of Manhattan – but it did not match such lofty aspirations.

'Madonna has been made up and costumed to look like an aspiring bag lady with the skin of a pneumonia victim,' offered one of the more polite American critics. Her fans stayed away from the film. But they bought the album and the title-track single which became an international hit. Don't cry for Madonna quite yet, appeared to be the message. She fobbed off the critics. She had learned from the film. Nikki has cleared her name and that was important. Madonna said she was always having to do that with the public.

Penn was not helping. He had gone out to dinner at the West Beach Café in Venice with a blonde girl and had been spotted by photographers who patrol such celebrity hangouts. Why don't stars like I-want-to-be-left-alone Penn eat dinner at home? That night, cameraman Cesare Bonazza wished he had. He claims that after he took some pictures of Penn and the unknown girl the actor chased after him in his truck.

He jumped from the truck and yelled: 'Come out of the car you mother-fucker!' He reached under his T-shirt and pulled out a gun. He got in a shooting position with both hands grabbing the gun and pointed at me. He said: 'Give me the fucking camera, give me the fucking camera.' He was crazy, a lunatic.

Bonazza says he did not take a picture of Penn threatening with the gun because he feared that the threat could turn fatal. 'I couldn't believe the guy, one of these days he's going to get killed. I was just lucky to escape him in the traffic.'

Another day, another brawl. This time a more far-reaching incident involving Penn. He was working for reformed Hollywood bad boy, Dennis Hopper, on the film *Colors* and co-starring with Robert Duvall. The actors played veteran/young lion cops in the film about Los Angeles street gangs. For an article on the gangs, whose territory spreads across many of the sporting venues used for the 1984 Olympics, I had spent several frightening weeks on their 'turf'. *Colors* was to me a grand and accurate picture of the horror and squalid and violence in gang life. But to make it on location, using gang members for most of the extras? Madonna made three very secret visits to Penn during location filming. Hopper told me:

All the gang members knew Sean – they'd all seen *Bad Boys*. They'd say: 'Hey, man, we know you're playing a cop but we don't know, you know.' They thought he was one of them. One of the Mexican gangs – the White

Fence Gang – asked him to sign a homeboy [gang member] symbol for them. He said: 'I don't want to sign that.' They couldn't understand and asked him why. He said: 'Because my homeboys are the Los Angeles Police Department.' He was aggressive about that too.

The film's producer was the soft-spoken Robert Solo, who had cast Penn in *Bad Boys*. Sitting in a Hollywood hotel, he said:
I have always like Sean Penn and I have always had a great admiration for him. You know, when they were making the film they were in jeopardy a lot. I think most of the crew were carrying weapons. People were getting killed nearby while we were filming. One of the gang members we were using on the film was called 'Destroyer' and Dennis asked him why. The 'Destroyer' guy told him: 'Sometimes I gotta do my business.' Sean and Dennis didn't have any protection but their images. The gang-bangers [gang members] liked them. 'Hey, Sean Penn. Hey, Sean Penn.' The image sticks. It's hard to remove.

Penn himself talked to me about Madonna's visits and said that even in that most violent arena he was not concerned for her or his own safety:
We all have a certain sense of our ability to be and not to be bull-shitted. I think I can pretty well tell when someone is being who they are around me and when they're not. So, if I was going to say something good about these guys it's that they stay pretty much as close to who they are no matter who they are talking to as about anybody I've never met. That is that everything they say is a lie.

In *Colors* his cop character was called 'Pac Man' because he eats up the streets. What was his definition of masculinity?

'My definition for what?' he mugged. 'I can only say for the character.' Go on. 'In a world full of cunts, I'm the guy who can make sure the manhood stays around. That's what.'

It was during the filming of *Colors* that Penn not only landed himself in trouble, but in jail. It was in April 1987, a clear spring day out by the Pacific at Venice Beach. Jeffrie Klein, a scrap-metal dealer from Orange County – an hour's drive but decades in mentality from Hollywood – was one of a couple of hundred non-union extras getting $35 a day to fill out background scenes along Ocean Front Walk. One scene called for Hopper to film

Duvall and Penn strolling along. As they approached Klein, he took a camera from his jacket pocket and took some souvenir snaps. The camera lens was the red flag to Penn and he dashed towards Klein swearing and shouting: 'What are you doing taking pictures?' he screamed at Klein.

Six-foot tall and weighing 210 pounds, Klein explained he was an extra and that other people were also snapping pictures. 'Sean Penn then spat in my face and said: "What are you going to do now?" ' Klein spat back. Penn started a series of punches to Klein's face. Three times the crowd of extras separated the two of them and three times Penn broke free and went back to the attack. Meagan Montgomery, another extra there that day, recounts: 'I saw Penn try to leap over security guards and try to hit Klein on the head with his fist.'

It had only been two weeks since Penn was fined and put on probation for the Wolinski incident. This was a blatant breach of probation, although Penn's lawyer Howard Weitzman, who had won freedom for John DeLorean in his drug-trafficking case, argued that his client had not broken probation. It was a right mess and Madonna was distraught. She had a husband who thought he was a heavyweight contender. He was also a champion boozer. A few weeks later he was stopped for running a red traffic light; a blood test showed an alcohol content of slightly over .11 per cent, then a little over California's legal limit. The charge was reckless driving, another probation violation.

For weeks, Penn was to play cat and mouse with the press and the California authorities. And to sour the mix even more, Madonna said publicly that they were having marital problems. It looked like her marriage was going to turn out like her most recent films, rather miserable learning experiences.

Even before Penn went to court to be sentenced for the probation violations, she had determined that the marriage was over. Publicly, she was still standing by him.

ELEVEN

MADONNAMANIA

'Drugs never made anything easier to cope with. I don't do drugs because I like to be in control of my life.'

MADONNA IN 1987

While Penn prepared for his court appearance and juggled his commitment to film his father Leo's *Judgement in Berlin* on location in Germany, his wife was taking total control of her career. She had had eleven consecutive Top Five singles – only the Beatles and Elvis had matched that – and she wanted to build on that with her *Who's That Girl?* world tour and the release of the film. In long strategy meetings which would start at breakfast and often not finish until around midnight, she and her advisers were working on a new sweep of Madonnamania. She had trained for it. Two hours a day – everyday.

Behind Fortress Malibu, there had been some additions: a dance studio and a personal home gym with a trampoline and swimming pool as well as weights and other sweat tools. She

would take a bike out and spin up and down Pacific Coast Highway or go for runs at Pepperdine University. She was twenty
pounds lighter, trim and muscled and her bustier cinched even
tighter. To go with a new svelte body, she had new hair – the
Marilyn look. Although she was one of the best-selling recording
artists in the world and the seventh highest earning – $26 million
in 1987 – she was still desperate to escape her continuing image as
simply a media curiosity, a bimbo who got lucky. That same drive
that got her through the early days was propelling her forward
now.

Penn had got himself in a jam and he would have to cope. For
her, it must have seemed at the time that someone at Warner
Brothers Studios, who were releasing the *Who's That Girl?* film,
was psychic, for it would have been just too much had it retained
the original title of *Slammer*. Penn was sentenced for sixty days for
his probation violations. There were all kinds of rows and outcries
when the California courts agreed to allow him to spend the time
in two sessions so he could complete *Judgement in Berlin*. Now, he
was seen at a Beverly Hills restaurant and then strolling down
Fifth Avenue in New York with Madonna. They went to Mari-
gold's restaurant for lunch, window-shopped along Madison
Avenue and visited a well-known lingerie shop. Penn should have
been in Germany.

Arrest warrants were issued and then cancelled. The City
Fathers of Los Angeles demanded to know what was going on. It
was all a farce. Finally, Penn did serve thirty-two days of his
sentence in the spit of a town called Bridgeport (pop. 500) in
California's Mono County near the Mammoth Lake ski country.
Penn paid $80 a day to go to jail there rather than do his time in
the Los Angeles County Jail. The difference in conditions would
have had a more likely market value of $8000 a day. The food was
hot but not *haute*, the blankets grey but not Ralph Lauren gray. In
California, such sentences for bad boys and girls in show business
are laughingly called 'celebrity diversion programmes', much as
corporate offenders serving their time in open prisons known
as Club Feds. Nevertheless, for an edgy, nerve-driven energy

freak like Penn, any sort of confinement must have been hard to take.

Madonna was in Japan with her *Who's That Girl?* tour when Penn was sentenced.

Madonnamania? More than they ever expected. Thousands of fans stood outside the stadium in Osaka. Ticket touts wanted $700 a seat in Tokyo. Storms shut down the first show, but the fans did not go home. They stood outside her hotel in the rain and chanted her name. On stage, she did not disappoint. She was all energy in her clinging, skimpy black corset and fish-net stockings; then she changed to giant sun-glasses and a feather boa over black pants. Her intense preparation showed when she used Japanese phrases to encourage the audience to sing and dance with her. Later, two geishas made her up in traditional style. In return, she taught them how to wink and blow a kiss. She jogged for ninety minutes every day and also did much sightseeing, going unnoticed under a dowdy brown wig. The Far East was more fun this time, and she could finally bury the ghost of *Shanghai Surprise*. But every day Sean Penn was on the phone.

Madonna was enjoying herself alone. The tour was such an instant success, one she had worked for; it proved to her that her ethic of hard work and preparation did pay off. Penn she thought of as a dedicated and 'honest' actor. But hadn't she really married her image of him? The reality of the flying fists and boozing was a wedge between them. It had sent her from their home; she had spent nights in hotels only a half-hour drive from Malibu. Or she would take off to New York and the apartment. But now it was not so easy to hang out with the gang from the past. The days of anonymity were long gone.

She made her first chat-show appearance with America's king of that format, Johnny Carson, to promote her upcoming tour of the United States. She put on a brave face and played the flirt telling Carson: 'I'm just a Midwestern girl in a bustier,' and then added: 'I figured if I was going to present myself as a virgin to anyone it should be you.' Carson shot back: 'I suppose there has to be a first in my life.' It got the intended laughs.

Yet it was a sad time for Madonna. Professionally, she was getting it right. More than two million people on three continents would see her and adore her and lust after her. Privately, though, she had no answers in the weeks running up to her second wedding anniversary.

Martin Burgoyne, who had attended her wedding and with whom she had shared an apartment and her life in the New York days – he danced in her first video – had died of AIDS. He was a bartender at the Russian Tea Room when she was the hat-check girl. When Burgoyne had been diagnosed as having AIDS, his old friend had insisted on paying his hospital bills. She supported Burgoyne all through the illness. 'I still cry when I think of him,' she says. There were dark clouds all around.

She decided to take control. The United States' leg of her tour was to start in Miami. It took a 747 jet and a DC-7 to get the equipment from Tokyo to Florida and required twenty-three trucks to transport the specially built steel stage. It took a crew of about fifty technicians to set up. Coati Mundi of Kid Creole and the Coconuts was close with her: 'She's very conscious of how something looks. She likes to be in control of things. She pays 1001 per cent attention to everything.'

Out on Turnberry Island, a hedonist island on the Florida waterways where one-time presidential-hopeful Gary Hart was to get aboard the *Monkey Business* with Donna Rice and lose his White House chance, and where Dennis Thatcher likes to golf, the *Who's That Girl?* tour group set up luxury camp. Madonna brought an extra person – her husband. Penn played the suitor plying Madonna with white roses and orchids. Even when photographers tried to move in, Penn gently moved Madonna and himself out of range. He even said 'thank you' to a cameraman who asked to take his picture. Slugaholics do not reform overnight, but the riot act had been read.

Nevertheless, Penn resented the close contact between Madonna and the crew on the tour. They had their private jokes.

One regular Madonna worker revealed: 'We gave his wife a lot of attention and care and he resented that. Sean thought Madonna should be treated like everyone else's wife and she resented that. It always ended with everyone feeling awkward when he was around.' Penn had to leave Miami, finish his film, and go to jail. The bombardment of flowers continued. And the phone calls as Madonna performed her way across North America. One crew member says that while they were having a tactics meeting Penn got through to the switchboard of her hotel in Washington. Madonna kept him on hold for forty-five minutes. That is control. And confidence. Penn, who had said he did not care who wore the pants in his house as long as he took them off, could have pondered that while he was filming in Europe.

It was not long before the geography changed if not the attitude. Penn in jail in the California countryside of Mono County – strip searched, deloused and wearing a blue prison uniform stating Mono County Jail – was allowed fifteen-minute phone calls. Between the ones from his wife, he wrote a one-act play, *The Kindness of Women*, which he later directed on stage in Los Angeles. It is the story of a man involved in a stormy marriage involving sexual flings and heavy drinking. The dialogue ('You jerk', 'You bitch') sounded close to home. Penn admitted to me that it was.

Madonnamania was sweeping Europe. In Britain, fans swooned and louts demanded: 'Show us your tits.' Bodyguards and photographers jogged along after her. Not with her. She was in control this time. There would be no more *Shanghai Surprise* surprises. In France, she got involved in the politics of Premier Jacques Chirac, who for popularity reasons suddenly got interested in rock 'n roll. 'Everybody likes you very, very much,' he told her. 'I like you too,' said Madonna. Chirac hugged her and the fun began. 'Who's that girl at the side of the gentleman?' was the picture caption in the Paris tabloid, *Libération*. While an editorial about rock singers and politics asked: 'Who's that girl?' and replied: 'That girl is Jacques Chirac.' The debate roared on with other papers joining in.

What astonished the people of Paris even more was Madonna's eating habits. She was actually on two baked potatoes a day and popcorn, but for a 'banquet' dinner she served up clear turtle soup, avocado mousse and a choice of white wine or Perrier. A choice? She told her dinner guests: 'You didn't think I was going to sit here and watch you eat fancy food that I can't eat?' She was not so ungenerous in the Old Country.

'*Siete gia caldi?*' (Are you hot?) '*Allora, andiamo!*' (Then let's go) got her cheers of approval in Florence as The *That* Girl, as the roadies now called the tour, blasted through Italy. In Turin, Madonna met members of the family of her second cousin Amelia Vitucci, who gave her a painting of the original family home in Pacentro. Madonna was delighted. She did a little jump of a two-step and turned to eleven-year-old Giuseppe Vitucci and asked: 'Do you want to dance with me?' The crowd did, but the young boy was not sure and showed embarrassment as he told her: 'I don't know.' His mother Amelia later said it was one 'of the wonderful moments', and added: 'Her family left Pacentro very poor. There was not work and it's magnificent that she came back to us like that, as a great lady, a great success. Her family must be very proud.'

Bambina de Guilio was then Madonna's closest relative in Italy. She was eighty-two in 1987, but has since died. She was not well enough to make the journey from Pacentro in Turin with the seven town councilmen who did. They gave her a parchment proclamation as an honorary citizen of their town. When photographers crowded around her and her distant relatives, there was no problem. Madonna turned to everyone and said: '*Formaggio.*' [Cheese.] While Madonna was playing to standing-room-only crowds – in Turin a dozen people were injured in the crush to ogle her – an enterprising Italian journalist went for a drink with some of the folks in Pacentro. He quoted one customer as saying over sips of grappa: 'That girl sings and dances and shows her thighs. She is a *malafemina* [loose woman]. No Madonna she. The devil is more like it.'

It may have been simply the location, but then talk started

about Madonna and a connection with organized crime. There were said to be investigations going on. But enquiries show that most police activity involving background checks were on Sean Penn. What alarm bells may have gone off during such enquiries are not on file in Detroit, Los Angeles, or New York. An investigator in Los Angeles said that he had heard the stories which said that Madonna had been bankrolled by other than legitimate sources to launch herself and that there was a long on-going connection. In New York, the Mafia watchers and – unofficially – the investigators said there had been gossip, but nothing more than that. It is clear there never was.

A prisoner who shared a cell with Penn says that Madonna talked every day on the phone with him. There were calls from France and Italy. But when she got to Malibu, there was silence. She was busy. There were several 'heated' phone chats before Madonna made it to Mono County Jail. Other inmates had got him going with stories about her being out on the town with Cher and Sheena Easton. On her first visit, they argued. Twenty minutes later, she stormed out. When Penn was released, Madonna made lots of optimistic noises. They went to a marriage counsellor. She started house-hunting, telling the Beverly Hills realtors of Hyland, Young and Alvarez she wanted a place of her own. Elaine Young, once the wife of the late actor Gig Young, reveals: 'There was not a question it was a place for a bachelor girl.'

Then she stopped house-hunting. Madonna was convinced she was pregnant. She and Penn had been celibate during her tour and his jail time. She was sure that all that self-denial had resulted in something 'cosmic' and positive when they did get together. But shy of publicity about this, she made her 'medical' decision on a home-pregnancy test kit. It was wrong as her gynaecologist on Rexford Avenue in Beverly Hills quickly discovered. No baby – well, then no marriage.

Sean Penn was on the road alone. As a surprised newspaperman found out.

In Los Angeles, the film critic for the Santa Monica *Evening*

Outlook was driving out to the Pacific Coast from a movie screening. He saw a rather bedraggled sad-looking chap thumbing for a lift. He stopped and asked: 'Where are you going?' 'Malibu,' said Sean Penn who was hitching his way around town, fearful of another spell in jail if he dared to drive a car without insurance. Penn was hitting the bars of Malibu and Venice Beach. He was seen with friends and girls. The cameramen loved this. Madonna spent Thanksgiving in New York with some of her family and without Penn.

After being out of touch for four days, her husband turned up late in New York looking for his celebratory turkey dinner with all the trimmings. The story was that instead she served him divorce papers. In reality, after discovering she was not pregnant, she decided to go ahead with the divorce. When Penn turned up that Thanksgiving, she announced her decision but did not start talking to lawyers until the following week. She went public with it too, saying the divorce was not the result of one incident but 'a series of cumulative pressures'. Liz Rosenberg, the Warner Brothers' publicity person who has supported Madonna for years, then explained: 'There were so many moments in their marriage when it was shaky that Madonna was finally forced to face the reality of the situation – that they weren't happy together.'

The best career move since losing her virginity, laughed the wags. Loyal Rosenberg rebutted: 'She wanted the marriage to work. All the jokes about the marriage motivated her to work hard to making the marriage go. I don't think she considered him in terms of her career.'

An unhappy Penn sloped off to Los Angeles. Madonna stayed with her sister Paula out in Brooklyn. Penn went to Helena's. British singer Billy Idol was at the bar with photographer Vinnie Zuffante (Penn had hit him the previous year) and as drinks went down, so Penn's ire went up. Finally, he demanded that Helena, a long, dark-haired Greek woman careful of her celebrity clientele, throw Zuffante out even though he was without a camera.

Penn went off to the bathroom but saw the queue and decided against waiting. He went outside and peed against the wall of the building. Normally he would have reacted differently and drowned his sorrows in yet more drink and violence. He did not. It was certainly a different way for Penn to behave. And probably the best way for within a couple of weeks Madonna dropped the divorce action. It was later nullified. And Penn would sit in the Hollywood hotel saying of the lawsuit: 'The divorce was more for the magazines than reality. Making any family work is an endless job that's hard enough when the family isn't public.' But for the couple who had married their images it had been, as Penn was to discover, rather like peeing into the wind, despite the efforts of James Foley.

It was James Foley, the director who had worked with and admired both Penn and Madonna in their separate ways, who had brought about the reconciliation. While the lawsuit was still being pursued, they began talking on the telephone. Their conversations got longer. Foley encouraged them. Then, Penn promised Madonna something he had always written off as simply for wimps. He would see a marriage counsellor, whenever she wanted him to. The boozing would stop, the punching days were over . . . this was a promise-her-anything reconciliation. Over Christmas, they renewed their marriage vows. It was their last Happy Christmas together. And it was going to be a rocky New Year for the woman who had become one of the best-known entertainers in the world.

TWELVE

BAD MEMORIES

'I could never live a sheltered life – that would drive me insane.'

MADONNA IN 1988

———

The rains came early to southern California in 1988. The storm clouds swept in from the Pacific one after the other as Madonna tried to settle back into marriage and concentrate again on her career. Her annual pre-tax earnings were around $25 million and Henry Scolinos, a Los Angeles lawyer who was involved in a contract lawsuit with her, marvelled: 'I'd take her street-smart business sense over someone with a Harvard MBA any day. What she lacks in a formal business education, she more than makes up for with street smarts.' Madonna's discipline is more than a dancer's or a businesswoman's. It is the discipline of a driven workaholic. Her appearance is a business asset – she works out for three hours every day. There are hours to be creative, to write songs, work out routines, read film scripts and plan tours. There are hours for business on her fax machines and multi-line Merlin phone systems. But were there also enough hours in the day for her marriage? A good Catholic girl should always find time for marriage.

She and Penn were certainly trying. But whether they were star-crossed or not, they could not stay away from publicity. And it was not anything to do with them. First, truck driver Steven Stillbower drove his pick-up through the front gate of their Malibu estate. He wanted to 'see' Madonna. Penn made a citizen's arrest. More worrying was an incident when the couple arrived home with her brother Mario at 12:30 a.m. They had been grocery shopping – at the all-night supermarket on Pacific Coast Highway – and found five people wandering around their property. Penn drove Madonna to the main house where she called the police. He drove back to close the gates and at the same time called the police on his car phone. Mario drove another car down to the gates to back up Penn. Malibu Deputy Sheriff Bill Wehner recalls the evening:

Sean, with the help of Mario, approached these guys and attempted to stop them. One of them tried to punch Sean, and Sean, looking to defend himself, found a bottle of tofu salad dressing he had just bought and hit the guy with it.

Tofu – isn't that bean curd? And that is a protein, non-animal type of thing. Blue cheese would have been very messy.

When the police reporters discovered the incident, the salad-dressing-Sean-Penn-brawl got the actor some of the most positive publicity he had ever had. But it was still publicity and more evidence that whatever happened in their lives would go on in the public spotlight.

Even Madonna's morbid fear of death was to become painfully public. She never expected to live longer than her mother, whom she had watched suffer and die so painfully from breast cancer. When Madonna discovered a lump on her left breast, she panicked. Initially she did the right thing and went for an examination. There were uneasy minutes in the South-West-style reception room of Dr Jerrold Steiner, a cancer specialist who treated the late Sammy Davis Junior and the late actress-comedienne Gilda Radner.

Steiner, a soft-spoken man with a salt and pepper beard, spent twenty minutes explaining the problems and treatments available for breast cancer before examining Madonna. After he did, he asked Madonna to return in two weeks for another examination and test at the Cedars-Sinai building in Los Angeles. For the first time in her life, Madonna ran away from the confrontation. She had seen her mother waste away and the haunting memories and possibilities for her were too agonising to deal with. Finally nearly a dozen weeks – months which in other circumstances could have proved fatal – she braved it out and after taking a mammogram, Steiner carried out a biopsy which proved negative.

There was some joy from Madonna's fears.

The cancer scare brought her and Penn closer together. They would entertain at home in Malibu. One of the guests was Scandanavian journalist Sindre Kartvedt. A serious film journalist, he was someone they could easily accept in their home. But Kartvedt says he was never really comfortable during the visits:

They both seemed to be playing out their roles. Sean was the husband. Madonna was the housewife. And neither role fitted them. They both had opinions. They both wanted to give their point of view. In that relationship, it was clear they could never be equals. They both felt as though they were more important than each other. She always seemed to be playacting. I think she enjoyed the role of the homemaker but that's all it was – a role. When you study her character – and there are all kinds of psychological theories – it makes me think that someone somewhere in her childhood may have abused her. All the insecurities, the need to be in control, to be the boss, fit that sort of psychological profile.

Indeed, what would Freud have interpreted from the Madonna-Penn union? It was an explosive match. 'I was raised to believe that when you marry someone you marry him for life. You never give up,' said Madonna. She also said something which pointed to Penn's bitterness over her success:

Sean used to make fun of me. You know, those cut-off jeans I wear? Sean would bring someone back to the house and I'd be wearing those with my hair all *yech* – I mean, I'd be looking like a hag. And he'd bring a friend in and drag me over and say, 'Look at her, she's one of the richest women in America.' There's a difference between being born into money and making money. I'm from a poor background and basically I'm still a working-class girl. I've been known to wash a dish or two, make a bed or two.

Penn was to go off to Thailand to co-star with Michael J. Fox in *Casualties of War*, a Vietnam drama to be directed by Brian De Palma. Penn said he would miss his wife but sighed: 'But we've been through worse things than that, I guess.'

Had they?

Credibility was what they both desperately wanted. Madonna was a big star and a big earner, but still wanted to prove she could act, and decided the place to prove it was Broadway, where they have been known to butcher veteran stage stars overnight. She had been a long-time fan of playwright (and film screenwriter and director) David Mamet. She had enjoyed his *Glengarry Glen Ross* which had won Mamet the Pulitzer Prize, but it was when she saw his film *House of Games* she decided he was a 'genius' and 'I knew I had to work with this man.' She went out and auditioned with more than 300 other would-be Broadway stars for the three-character drama *Speed-the-Plow*. Ron Silver and Mamet regular Joe Mantegna had already been cast as a couple of Hollywood sharks hustling a film deal. The female role is of a secretary 'temp' who becomes a pawn in a power game.

'I'd wake up every morning with butterflies in my stomach,' recalls Madonna of the days of *Speed-the-Plow*. The tickets were $35 a time – twice what Madonna fans would pay to see her in concert – for an orchestra seat at the Royal Theatre in New York. In the preview week the theatre was packed. Madonna on the Great White Way brought out autograph hunters, hustlers, memorabilia dealers, and even theatre-goers.

It was fifteen minutes before Madonna appeared on stage carrying a coffee tray. A year earlier she had been parading on stage in her underwear. But here, she was in dark hair, skirt, glasses and sensible shoes. Mantegna's character wants to take the 'temp' Karen to bed. Silver bets him $500 that he can't. The New York papers had fun, 'NO, SHE CAN'T ACT' shouted the *Daily News*. In Britain the *Guardian* – what would seem the most non-Madonna of newspapers – was more enthusiastic: 'She plays what looks like Mamet's version of the early Marilyn who also had an ambition to star on Broadway.'

Madonna only got her chance because first choice Elizabeth 'Big' Perkins dropped out suddenly. Director Gregory Mosher had helped Madonna in her only previous stage work, as a gangster's moll in a 1986 workshop production of David Rabe's *Goose and Tomtom*. When Madonna heard Perkins was no longer going ahead, she called Mosher and asked for an audition. 'Madonna didn't Bogart her way into the role,' remembers Joe Mantegna who plays a gaudy hoodlum in *Godfather III*, adding, 'A lot of high-powered actresses also auditioned.'

There were six weeks of rehearsals and the Madonna discipline of preparation and rehearsal kicked in. Ron Silver, who starred with Oscar-winner Jeremy Irons in *Reversal of Fortune*, recalls: 'She was funny and feisty and the first one to know her lines – a professional. I liked her moxie.' Vanessa Redgrave, who flew from London to see the show, sent on congratulations. Mosher says:

Madonna could have made a spectacle of herself, thrown her weight around or even tried to capitalize on her sexy image, but she didn't. She was a real actress – just right. She wasn't the Material Girl or her version of Marilyn Monroe.

At the opening night part at the Tavern on the Green, she appeared wearing a pale blue dress with pearls. It had a subdued effect and designer Marlene Stewart – always one for the moment – said it was entirely intentional.

But as often with Madonna, it was an illusion. She was nowhere as cool as she looked. Throughout the run of the show she had constant changes of costume. Even the dressers remarked – and two even complained – about the smell of her costumes, the stench from the perspiration. The fear of putting herself out there – what must have been an incredible pressure – she has always dismissed as 'butterflies'. It may have been one of her most terrifying stage appearances, but Lindsay Law, who was executive producer of her next film *Bloodhounds of Broadway*, said: 'It was one of the smartest things she'd ever done.'

Madonna worked with a string of established acting talents – Randy Quaid, Rutger Hauer, Matt Dillon, and Jennifer Grey – on *Bloodhounds* which was sort of a *Guys and Dolls* romp. Screenwriter and director Howard Brookner took four Damon Runyon short stories and set them over one night – New Year's Eve, 1928. The theme was death, near-death and the threat of death: a black comedy. Madonna's story involved Quaid, as Feet Samuels, who has agreed to sell his giant feet to a crazy doctor to pay off gambling debts. Then he learns Madonna's Hortense Hathaway loves him and life is not so bad. He wants to keep his feet. It was a small-scale project which retains an oddball charm. Madonna says she realized about half-way through filming that something was wrong with Brookner, who was later to die from AIDS. In turn, he asked her about watching her friend Martin Burgoyne die from AIDS. The theme of *Bloodhounds* and the tragic reality – an eerie surrealism, a Fellini movie – made Madonna her most reflective about sexuality. About risks. About how far you, or rather she, could go. About homosexuality. About lesbianism.

Apart from this sexual dark side, *Bloodhounds* more happily gave her a friend in Jennifer Grey, the talented daughter of Joel (*Cabaret*) Grey, who had co-starred with Patrick Swayze in the runaway surprise hit, *Dirty Dancing*. Grey had broken up with actor-boyfriend Matthew Broderick and, with Penn on location in the Far East, there were many girls-nights-out.

Grey took her new friend to a birthday party for Sandra Bernhard, the off-beat actress who had slipped into the mainstream in Martin Scorcese's *King of Comedy*, co-starring with Robert De Niro. Madonna liked Bernhard's cool, caustic humour and went to see her one-woman show *Without You I'm Nothing*. Much of Bernhard's act is playing out fantasies. The evening Madonna was in the audience, Bernhard told a joke about how she and Madonna survived World War III: the punchline was that Penn

did not, which got lots of laughs at the time because of the publicity surrounding their relationship. It was the start of an on-
going and controversial friendship with all the talk of them enjoying an active lesbian relationship. And it was Midwest girls
together. Bernhard was another escapee from Michigan, from
Flint, another Motor Town sprawl. Relate? These ladies were
almost related.

Sandra Bernhard provided a shoulder for Madonna through
the last gruelling months of her marriage. The performer, a couple
of years older than Madonna and known as The Mouth That
Roars, is tall (5 ft. 10 in.) and skinny (7 stone, 12 lb.) and when
she recalls how they became best friends, she remembers the
moment: 'I was talking to her on the phone and I said, "I can't
imagine being you." And she said, "I can't imagine being you." I
thought that was a very nice thing to say.'

By now they were quite literally bosom buddies. Wearing
matching sequined bras, they bumped and ground on stage belting out Sonny and Cher's 'I Got You Babe' at a benefit concert in
New York. When the on-stage fondling got a little too much for
the celebrity audience, which included Glenn Close and Meryl
Streep, the high-spirited Madonna screamed: 'Don't believe those
stories.'

Leering into the microphone, the other side of this new
dynamic duo shouted: 'Believe those stories!' Which is absolutely
Sandra Bernhard's style. She does not simply light up a room –
she just takes it over.

I'm a control person. It's hard for me to relinquish my power. It's like my
weight – I'm counting down. I want to look like I'm needy because I am. We
all are. It's just what I need, I don't want.

I need stardom. It's part of the package. I wouldn't choose it on its own
but in order to do what I do, I've gotta get people to pay to see me.

I'm coming from a million places. I create a persona – the ravenous
predator.

She is certainly unpredictable as many American talk-show hosts
have found. One minute she has got the talk-show host and his
audience wildly laughing – and then she will drop a silencing line:

'Joni Mitchell hasn't left the Malibu Colony in ten years and here she is singing about Ethiopia.'

She was born in America's car country of Michigan. But raised in the country-club country of Scottsdale, Arizona, where every other open space is a golf course. Her mother was an abstract artist: 'We didn't join the country club – my mother thought it was pretentious. It's because of that, I never had a nose job and consequently became the girl I wanted to be.'

At eighteen, she moved to Los Angeles and got her job as a manicurist working on the fingers and toes of celebrities: 'I did Dyan Cannon one time. She never looked at me as I dug the sand from under her big toenail.' While she polished and buffed all day, at night, she worked the town's famous comedy clubs. On and on and on for eight years. The big moment came with Martin Scorcese's *The King of Comedy*, where Jerry Lewis, *the* Jerry Lewis, played a television talk-show host who is kidnapped by Robert De Niro and Bernhard, as a crazy in her underwear. She had arrived. Her notices for the film were sensational. Her career decisions not so good. She turned down *Ghostbusters* which is still the biggest-earning comedy ever ('Not a good move,' she deadpans), but was a sadistic nurse in Nicolas Roeg's *Track 29*.

She is a great fan and a loyal friend to Madonna. 'We have fun, we enjoy each other's company. What more do you want me to say about it? Yes, we're best friends. And being a best friend is always being around when your friend needs you.' Bernhard says that despite their hard-edge approach, both she and Madonna are 'vulnerable'. She confesses:

I am a serious manic depressive. I get tired of being sarcastic. People think I'm always sarcastic. I try to get off in different ways, being funny, but sarcasm is very easy for me. It's the easy way to make people laugh – or being wild, being really wild. Actually, I like that better.

She has been called many, many things – even pretty. She does not agree:

I don't consider myself pretty. Pretty means something helpless, something unattainable and unreachable, and I don't think I'm that way.

I think I'm sensual, I'm more beautiful than I am pretty. Pretty is a high-school cheerleader. I learned early the advantage of being funny. I knew how to make people laugh, to manipulate them. I'm not the type that gets into something and drops my own persona. I'm more of an observer and a commentator. I've never done drugs. I hate it. I like being really lucid. I like being in control. When people try to give me drugs, it's sloppy, it's ugly and its inexcusable behaviour. I stand for total freedom and just live my life in an honest way. I'm open to a lot of different things. I mean, a girl likes to have a good time. But I don't like to classify myself. I want people just to not know what's going on. To be a little confused and irritated and say, 'Who does she think she is?' That's fine.

The madcap lady who likes biker leathers, Bon Jovi, Prince, seventies disco, leather bustiers, glitter bras, and Madonna, would also like to have a child. Adoption is not an option: 'I'd rather have my own child. Better breeding. Better quality control.' And Madonna? 'She's my best friend – not my gynaecologist.'

Bernhard did get a little irritated over some of the talk about her and Madonna's 'close' relationship and uncharacteristically reacted with:

We're friends and that's it. The press just can't be happy when two cool girls like us are tight buddies – like no competition, no bitchiness, except that mock stuff we put on, kind of like Dean Martin and Jerry Lewis.

By the way: did anyone ever accuse Dean and Jerry of getting it on? No. The press have to turn it into some freaky, sordid scandal when they *should* be highlighting the fact that maybe for once, two strong women are setting a positive example for the rest of the gals – it's fine to be supportive of your girlfriends, like not all women are back-stabbing, vicious nightmares. So everyone in the press can kiss my fat butt.

I asked Bernhard about this outburst at a Beverly Hills reception. 'Oh, that? Haemorrhoids, I suppose.'

In 1991, Madonna also got testy about their relationship. She was also most revealing:

Sandy's a great gal. Sandy's one of my only girlfriends, really. She's one of the only girls that can take me. She's really a ballsy girl. Most girls just hide under the couch. We frighten everyone out of the room. Sandy and I have always been great friends. I think in the very beginning there was a flirtation, but I realized I could have a really good friend in Sandra, and I wanted to maintain the friendship. When I went on the David Letterman Show, it wasn't exactly clear how things were going to go. But Sandy started playing up that we were girlfriends, and I thought, *Great, OK, let me go for it.* Because, you know, I *love* to fuck with people. Just as people have pre-conceived notions about gay men, they certainly do about gay women. So if I could be some sort of a detonator to that bomb, then I was willing to do that. It was really fun.

Then, of course, it went highly out of control. Everybody picked up on it, and the question was, are we sleeping together? It's not really important. The fact is that Sandra sleeps with men too, and I think maybe she's trying to find happiness in her life. Maybe she was just thinking, *Can everybody just shut up so I can find somebody to have a decent relationship with?* Sandra's one of the most open people I know. You should see her in public. She's not trying to hide anything. I think it's ludicrous that people are accusing her of being in the closet or ashamed of being gay.

The fact is, she's a great friend of mine. Whether I'm gay or not is irrelevant. Whether I slept with her or not is irrelevant. I'm perfectly willing to have people think that I did. You know, I do not want to protest too much. I don't care. If it makes people feel better to think that I slept with her, then they can think it. And if it makes them feel safer to think that I didn't, then that's fine too. You know, I'd almost rather they thought that I did. Just so they could know that here was this girl that everyone was buying records of, and she was eating someone's pussy. So there.

While the world was fascinated by the Madonna-Bernhard-do-they-or-don't-they antics, Madonna was obsessed with another story – that of *Evita*. It would drive her for the next few years. With her Siren Films Company, she was negotiating a deal with Dawn Steel, then the president of Columbia Picturers. She and Siren development director, Stephanie Stephens, expected to have seven films 'in full swing' by 1989. The plan then was for a musical built around Madonna, dramatic roles and a comedy.

But when director Oliver Stone, hot from *Platoon* and *Wall Street*, flew into New York he had another offer – *Evita*. Stone arrived from California to screen test Madonna for the role of

Right: Express Yourself video, 1989
(Katz Eyes)

Below: On stage during the
Who's That Girl Tour in 1987
(LFI)

Above: Madonna shows off her agility during her first appearance in Europe, in 1982 *(Joe Bangay)*

Below: Playing 'Karen' on Broadway in *Speed the Plow*, 1988 (*Frank Spooner*)

Above: Shopping in New York, 1990, with Warren Beatty *(LFI)*, and *above right:* Out on the town in LA in the same year *(Sygma)*

Right: With Warren Beatty and Charlie Kors at the Washington DC premiere of *Dick Tracy* in June 1990 *(Frank Spooner Pictures)*

Left: Arriving at the 1991 Academy Awards with Michael Jackson *(LFI)*

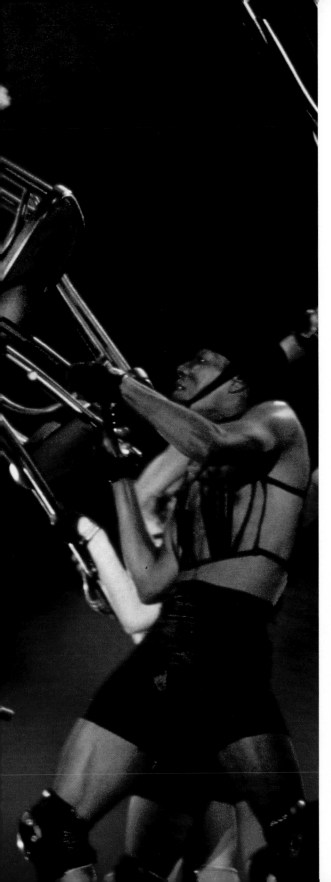

Three dramatic costume changes during the Blonde Ambition Tour in 1990 (Left: *All-Action Pictures;* below: *Sygma;* bottom: *LFI*)

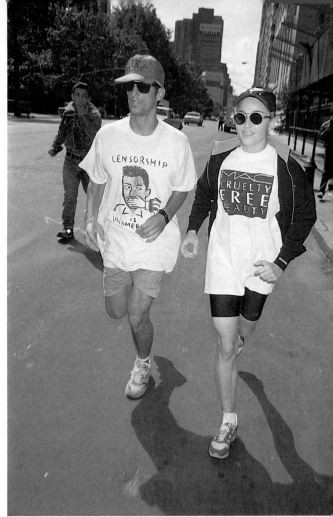

Above: With Tony Ward at the
Goodfellas premiere in New York,
September 1990 *(Sygma)*, and,
right: Seen jogging together a
month later *(Scope Features)*

Above: At the Paris fashion collections in October 1990 *(UK Press)*

Above: Lasting at the Dance
Marathon in May 1991 *(LFI)*

Above: With Alex Keshishian, the
director of *Truth or Dare,* and
brother Christopher, at the
film's premiere in New York,
1991 *(LFI)*

Left: May 1991, in Cannes *(LFI)*

Left: May 1991, in Cannes *(LFI)*

From the documentary film
Truth or Dare, which was released
in Britain with the controversial
title, *In Bed With Madonna*
(Frank Spooner Pictures)

Juan Peron's wife, the 'saint' who died of cancer in her thirties. Elaine Paige and others involved in the Andrew Lloyd-Webber/Tim Rice stage spectacular were not so sure. Streisand had been mentioned for the role. Meryl Streep had made a demonstration singing tape for Lloyd-Webber and Rice. During an interview, I asked her to sing a few bars of 'Don't Cry For Me Argentina' and she burst into a fit of giggles and said: 'I can't go to London. Elaine Paige would kill me.'

But Streep, who was later to be devastated by not getting the *Evita* role, should not have been Paige's target. Madonna was the one in line for the role. But she told Stone she would not screen test. It was an absurd gesture. Stone, who would go on to *Born on the Fourth of July*, *The Doors* and *JFK*, is himself a strong personality. It appeared to be a Mexican stand-off. However, Madonna was determined. One day *she* would be 'Evita'. As always, she was in the overachieving business.

She was also still trying to be Mrs Penn. Her husband was appearing in the play *Hurlyburly* in Los Angeles where Madonna was a regular at rehearsals and would telephone much of the time. But on opening night, she was late. And she arrived with Sandra Bernhard. Later in the evening, at a Century City club near the theatre, Penn was back to being the bad boy: 'You cunt. How could you do this to me?' he was heard shouting at Madonna.

As 1988 headed to a conclusion, so did their fiery marriage. A former employee at their Malibu home reveals how far things had gone. They would argue all the time, with Penn punching out doors and walls or taking off into the grounds to shoot rabbits and birds, 'anything that moved'. He twice shoved Madonna into their swimming pool. Penn, according to the employee, would also brag about his affairs with beach girls. Guns were hidden around the house. The maids had instructions to tell Madonna if they found any weapons.

But even with all this marital madness, she was still taking care of business. She knew all about Warren Beatty's *Dick Tracy* – she had been introduced to Beatty by Penn on their first date – and called him up asking for the role of Breathless Mahoney. Within a month, she was eating dinner at the Great Greek restaurant in Sherman Oaks just over the hill from Beatty's Mulholland Drive estate. Their dinner companion was former presidential hopeful and long-time Beatty friend, Gary Hart. Madonna had got her role and her man. She had also lost her other one.

The Madonna-Sean Penn marriage was over. Until now, the extent of her life as a 'battered wife' was not known. Colleagues, friends and associates of the couple would only talk about the wild days of their relationship with assurance of anonymity. They told fearful stories. Of how Madonna would always take the car keys with her so that if Penn got out of hand he was the one looking for a ride home. And how Penn's constant rages and outrageous tantrums killed any love Madonna had for him. And how they feared for her life if the rages got out of control.

As it did in the dying days of 1988. Madonna had agreed to work with Hollywood's leading Lothario, Warren Beatty, and even an easy-going spouse might have difficulty with that one. Penn reacted by leaving home and moving in with his parents four miles away down the Pacific Coast. He had spent Christmas with his family and out drinking with friends. She had gone to a party with some girlfriends. These were tense, estranged days.

It was just after 4 p.m. on 28 December when Penn broke into his own home. Madonna had allowed all the help time off for the holidays. Penn put Madonna through hours of terror. He hit her. He tied her up and he humiliated her. He also sexually assaulted her.

Officers involved in such cases are forbidden by Californian law to reveal exact details of certain sexual offences: these include acts against children and others involving adults. Lieutenant Bill McSweeney was with the Malibu Sheriff's Department at the time of the incident. He is now an officer with the Los Angeles County Sheriff's Internal Affairs in downtown Los Angeles. There, in his fourth floor office, he recalled how Madonna dealt with her humiliation and terror 'in a business-like way'.

Lieut. McSweeney would not specify the sexual offences Penn inflicted on Madonna other than telling me: 'It was a unique, specific type of violence.' He did indicate it was an act where Californian law is constructed to protect the privacy of victims. And under *Deering's Penal Code*, the Californian lawbook setting limits for sentences for various crimes, they are:

288a (Oral Copulation): When the act is accomplished against the victim's will by means of force or fear of immediate and unlawful bodily injury on the victim or another person.

289 (Penetration by any foreign object): Every person who causes the penetration however slight of the genital or anal openings of any person or causes another person to so penetrate another person's genital or anal openings for the purpose of sexual gratification by any foreign object, substance, instrument or device when the act is accomplished against the victim's will.

286 (Sodomy): Sodomy is sexual conduct consisting of contact between the penis of one person and the anus of another person.

264 (Rape): Rape is an act of sexual intercourse accomplished with a person not the spouse of the perpetrator.

Until now the stories surrounding Penn's 'torture' of Madonna have told of him slapping her about and threatening to cut off her hair. She was held captive for many hours, even days depending on what account you accept. But Lieut. McSweeney offered this view:

It was all over by the time we got there. The act had been completed.

It was a serious matter. It was something that if prosecuted would have had great implications. It was fully explained to her what charges she could bring.

Penn could not, as Madonna's husband, have legally raped her. McSweeney indicated he would have been charged with one or more of the three other offences.

Madonna had told Penn, who was slugging Stoli vodka from a bottle, that it was all over for ever. He tried to tie her to a chair in what was once their bedroom, but she got away. He grabbed her in the living room and bound her. His litany of 'bitch, slut, whore' banged about her head. And then there was the most awful humiliation.

Police are not sure how Madonna freed herself. One officer dismissed a suggestion that Madonna had 'seduced' her way out of the trouble explaining: 'It wasn't that sort of situation.' She called the police on her car phone. Later, at the Malibu Sheriff's office she appeared with her face awash in tears, her lip cut. But Lieut. McSweeney remembers that she was, despite her ordeal, very much in control and matter of fact about the official complaint she made against Penn. She was, he said, detailed and determined. And it was an act covered by the privacy code. He said,

When she turned up at the Malibu office to report what had happened, half of her was dispassionate. The other half was distressed. Her face was streaked with tears. She seemed to be making a business-like decision which she had made analytically. She seemed to have made up her mind, made her decision. She was in control and it's rare to find anyone who can cope like that in such circumstances. She was clearly distressed and anxious to report what happened.

There were no problems with Penn at the house. 'As far as I recall, he co-operated with the officers,' said Lieut. McSweeney.

The case changed in a few days: 'She seemed to have made another business decision. She seemed to have analysed the whole situation and decided which was the best way to take it.' Madonna had decided she did not want further humiliation – an ordeal that would be drawn out in court and fanfared by an international media circus if she pressed charges against Penn. To have made them in the first place reveals not how distraught and fearful she was, but how bloody angry she was at the humiliation, the outrage at being so brutally controlled.

The police wanted to take things further. But Madonna resisted their pressure and had a meeting with Los Angeles County's Deputy District Attorney, Lauren Weiss. The details of her assault report were sealed – until now. 'Madonna asked there be no criminal charges pressed. There was no other evidence on which to base a criminal charge so there wasn't one filed,' said Al Albergate, the official mouthpiece for the District Attorney's office. He did not say that behind the scenes there was pressure on Madonna to proceed.

But she stood by her 'business decision'. On 5 January 1989, in Los Angeles Superior Court, she filed for divorce citing 'irreconcilable differences'.

She had never returned to the Malibu home. Friends and help had retrieved her belongings. She never wanted to be inside the house again. Instead, she had found her $2.9 million hideaway in the Hollywood Hills. And within two weeks she and Penn – who had all manner of criminal charges hanging over his head if Madonna wanted to play hard ball with him – had agreed on a division of community property. He kept the Malibu estate, she held on to the New York apartment. Penn got a good deal because Madonna also paid him $498,000, which was his 'share' of the Manhattan apartment. He got their South-Western- and Santa Fe-style Malibu furniture, while she held on to the art deco and art nouveau paintings and sculptures. She left behind her gold wedding band, which had been inscribed 'M LOVE S', in her bathroom cabinet.

The financial end of their three and a half year marriage also revealed something of the cost of living as Mr and Mrs Madonna, the mundane and the costly side of stardom: $22.50 to the Southern California Gas Co., $60 to John's Rubbish Co., $36 to Western Exterminator Co., $88.98 to Sprint, $24.20 to the *Los Angeles Times* for newspapers, $348.42 telephone bill, $450 for a credit-card payment, $92.22 to Falcon Cable TV, $50 to Penn's mother, Eileen, for an IOU, $2,118.75 to a security-consultant firm, $225.50 to Bragg's Pool Service, $3,081.61 to an insurance broker, $6,000 to a 'tax-exempt fund', and $7,707.60 to an unnamed 'trustee'.

Penn's production company, Clyde Is Hungry Productions, Inc., issued thirty-one cheques totalling $62,223.35 for the month of September 1988, including: $125.06 to the LA Cellular Phone Co., $5,425.00 to his dentist, Henry R. Dwork, $59 to On the Rox Club on Sunset Boulevard, $700 to boyhood pal, Jeff Higginbotham, $1,829.95 to American Express, $2.026.36 to PMK, a Hollywood publicity company, $27,921.60 to Arnold & Porter, a New York law firm, $17,500 to Manatee and Co., a Los Angeles financial consulting firm, and the less grand sum of $49 to Burbank Self Storage Co.

Madonna left the bills, Penn and Malibu and moved on to Hollywood.

THIRTEEN

THE TOP
OF THE HILL

'I cry when I see the Wizard of Oz.

Every time. '

Madonna bought her new home from Allen Questrom, the Chief Executive of Neiman Marcus, the Texas-based upmarket and expensive department store chain. Her neighbours included former *Charlie's Angel,* Cheryl Ladd, and down the road, Dolly Parton. But Madonna was alone. She was at the top of the hill – literally. But alone.

By now arguably the best-known entertainer in the world, she lives a ten-minute drive from Hollywood's Sunset Strip. There are a couple of tight turns that lead to a narrow street that dead-ends in a cul-de-sac and the electrified gates to Madonna's home. You cannot see the contemporary-style building from the street. You identify yourself over the intercom and there is a buzz and the gates swing open. A uniformed guard – they rotate around the clock – sits in a car and watches visitors. There is lots of green around. Friends go in by the garage, around the 1957 Thunderbird and Mercedes 560SL, and into the house through the kitchen and breakfast area. There are lots and lots of floor-to-ceiling windows, but they face to the pool and the small garden area. From the front, you see brick wall. And it is also easy to see the attraction of the mix of security and serenity. An elaborate laser security system encircles the property, and if the beam is broken, the alarms blast immediately; there is no 'waiting time' to allow for mistakes.

This is not the home of a BOY TOY. It is elegant with an eclectic collection of furniture and art placed as much for pleasure as for the effect. Everything has its place. There is not one cluttered closet. The gowns are lined up in order. The black leather jackets all hang together as do the cut-off jeans. The black kidskin gloves are together and the black coats and, of course, the black lacy corsets. So are the identical lace-up wing-tip black boots. The black looks are reserved for the maids who do not clean too well. Madonna's assistants see that notes are left on the chrome taps in the bathroom for the maid: you have not polished enough.

To the left and right of the tiled entrance way is a different touch – Madonna's office. Bookshelves have been built in and there are her desks and files with phones and fax machines. This is where the chief operating officer of Madonna Incorporated carries out her business. When you step through from the office, you are immediately in the main room. There is the grand piano and hung on the ceiling is a gold-framed Langlois (originally painted for Versailles) with Hermes' loins dangling down. Above the white-painted fireplace is a 1932 Fernand Léger entitled *Composition*. Across the room from it is a self-portrait by Mexican legend, Frida Kahlo. (Madonna has emerged now as such a cross-cultural icon that when the austere *New York Times* reviewed an exhibition of Mexican art at the New York Metropolitan Museum they made a point in the first paragraph of saying the work of 'Kahlo, Madonna's favourite artist', was included.) A nude by Kahlo's controversial husband, Diego Rivera, hangs on another wall.

There is a photograph of boxer Joe Louis by Irving Penn and Man Ray's nude of Kiki de Monparnasse. A Tamara de Lempicka painting hangs in her bedroom which is white-painted and spartan. There is no headboard for the bed which seems to have simply been pushed up against the wall. There is her mother's photograph and the one of her in her mother's wedding dress. You need to walk through the bathroom/dressing room to get there which is clean and ordered with an open shower. An eighteenth-century Italian day bed and matching chairs sit beside her weight-lifting equipment and benches in front of the back-lighted glass closets. There is something gladiatorial about the room.

There are pictures throughout the house. Some by her favourite photographer, Herb Ritts. Others by Tina Modotti and Matt Mahurin. She is fascinated by Frida Kahlo, the puzzling artist and revolutionary, who has become a cult figure in the eighties – with a little help from Madonna who still plans to make a film of Kahlo's life. In the foyer of her home is a Kahlo painting called *My Life*. It shows Kahlo's mother giving birth. The bed sheets hide her head. What is seen are her open legs and the grown-up Kahlo's head appearing from her mother's vagina. 'If somebody doesn't like this painting, then I know they can't be my friend,' says Madonna.

It was her friend and brother Christopher, who is gay, who helped decorate the ten-room house. He said they looked at twenty-four other properties before making their 'find'. 'I wanted to avoid the overstuffed California look,' he says of his work, but quickly points out:

I refuse to be called a decorator. The house has the feeling of a grand New York penthouse except the view is better and there is a pool. We both love Italian furniture. It's grand without being gaudy like French furniture. Madonna and I were very close although we had become distant for about five years. It was difficult for me to find a niche in her world. We have a certain sibling dependency and we spend a lot of time fighting. Yet, we are each other's best critics.

But by now Madonna was careful about who was doing the criticizing. She had got out of her marriage and Malibu and was now in Hollywood and, most importantly, in control. When she was starting out, Dick Clark, America's dominant disc jockey (*American Bandstand*) and film/television producer, had asked her what she wanted to do when she grew up. She shot back: 'Rule the world.'

Well, by now she was at least ruling her world. Stories of her hard-headed, tough attitude began circulating. Pat Leonard, who had worked on her tours and records, has this thought: 'Madonna had learned that after you've been burned enough times, it's better to be a tyrant than to be a wimp and have people walk all over you.'

Madonna Incorporated comprised Boy-Toy for her music business; Slutco for videos and Siren for her films. 'It's a great feeling to be powerful. I've been striving for it all my life. I think that's just the quest of every human being – power.'

But in Hollywood, power has all sorts of definitions. She was going to be in *Godfather III*: she wasn't. She was going to play in David Lynch's *Wild At Heart*: she didn't. She was going to reprise the Marlene Dietrich role in *Blue Angel*: she hasn't, but the project is not forgotten. Dietrich has said she would like Madonna to play her in any biographical film. And *Evita* was always, always in her sights. She threw director Oliver Stone off track when she suggested she should write some new *Evita* songs with Andrew Lloyd-Webber. She maintains she was never given enough guidance of the Stone-Robert Stigwood-Lloyd-Webber project at that early-talking stage. And when the down word on Streep circulated, Madonna simply shrugged that it had nothing to do with her.

Jeffrey Katzenberg is the chairman of Walt Disney Studios and one of the shrewdest thinkers in Hollywood. This is a man interested in the bottom line. Period. He does not pander to stars. He would rather make movies with animals who do not talk back and do not bark on about how many millions they are worth. A pragmatic man. And a Madonna fan:

She has a very secure sense of her life and her business. As far as I can tell, she's always had a vision of exactly who she is – whether as an actress or a performer, or as a lyricist or a music producer, or as a businesswoman. And she's also had a strong-enough sense of it to balance it all. She's always evolving. She never stands still. Every two years she comes up with a new way of presenting herself, a new attitude, a new act, a new design. And every time, it's successful. There is a constant genesis. When something like this happens once, OK, maybe it's luck. Twice is coincidence. Three times is just remarkable talent. A kind of genius. And Madonna's on her fifth or sixth time.

Madonna's financial adviser, Robert Nichols, was putting her money into real estate and 'ultra safe' investments on which his client/boss insisted. Stephanie Stephens and others were involved in movie deals at Columbia. There were plans for records and tours. The performer who had rewritten the entertainment rules of the eighties was chasing towards the next decade – with one of the largest media campaigns ever orchestrated. Madonna signed a $5 million deal with Pepsi Cola which gave her more than double that amount of money in free publicity. Manager Freddy DeMann thought it a smart move: 'The reason I wanted to do it was because her base audience was so much broader than what record companies generally approach. No record company can spend the kind of money Pepsi was prepared to spend.' What DeMann did not expect was the tempest in the cola bottle.

On 1 March 1989, Pepsi, from their headquarters in Somers, New York, sent out word that the next day the biggest coup in advertising history was going to happen. More than 250 million people in forty countries were going to have the delight of hearing Madonna's title song from her unreleased *Like a Prayer*. The song entitled 'Make a Wish' was the centrepiece of a video showing her on a trip down memory lane. As she went back to her childhood the pleasures of Pepsi would be highlighted. It was a first in many ways but shrewd Madonna was most aware of one thing: the video going world-wide did not just showcase the soft drink but gave her unprecedented publicity.

Todd Mackenzie was the official spokesman for the Pepsi-Cola Company and he was not lost for hyperbole: 'The ad will air around the globe, all across Europe and the Philippines, Thailand, Japan, in South America as well as North America. Just about every TV set on the planet Earth will have that commercial on it.'

Oh, yes. As Freddy DeMann said when asked why he was pushing Madonna so hard: 'You can't take anything for granted.' Especially not Madonna. Her records were selling more than one million copies a week, but you don't just pump out more of the same, do you? Pepsi was riding on Madonna's popularity – it cost them another $5 million to put the commercial on television – but she also had her video of 'Like a Prayer'. In it, she cavorts in a black slip, wriggles between burning crosses, kisses a black saint and shows stigmata – the imagery is provocative and irreverent. But is it blasphemous? It was a wonderful mix – Madonna, sex and religion – for a hurricane of headlines by which Pepsi got splashed. It was a video certain to outrage those who feel comfortable brandishing picket signs, and who instinctively phone-in protests, which may, of course, have been the idea from the start.

In the video, Madonna enters an empty church where she is drawn to a statue of a young black man robed in white – behind bars. She lies down on a pew and is apparently overcome by a vision, while the statue comes to life. In this vision, the scenario of a recent crime is unveiled. A group of white thugs attacks and stabs a white woman, but a black man who comes to her aid is arrested. Madonna is then awakened from her vision by a raucous black choir marching through the church. She goes to the local jail, where she vouches for the failed man's innocence before the police – standing at the sergeant's desk wearing only a brassière and a slip.

Madonna sings in front of a field of burning crosses. Madonna handles the murder weapon, a knife, and suddenly is supernaturally afflicted with bleeding nail wounds in her palms. Madonna does an uninhibited, giddy little dance with a gospel troupe, and at one point gets down on her knees while a choir member puts a hand on Madonna's forehead, faith-healer-style.

Rather than fall backwards from the healing touch, Madonna appears as if she might be about to fall out of her bra.

The video began running on MTV the day after the Pepsi commercial appeared on America's NBC TV. The picket signs went up. The phones rang – especially at Pepsico, makers of the soft drink and owners of fast-food chains like Kentucky Fried Chicken. Roman Catholic Bishop, Rene Gracids, of Texas and the American Family Association, called the video offensive. They called for a Pepsi and Pepsico product boycott. Madonna went pop. Pepsi yanked the commercial off the air.

The Pepsi commercial was the first time Madonna had agreed to tout or shrill a product. Michael Jackson, Paula Abdul and Bill Cosby could go their corporate way, but not Madonna. She feared it might compromise her artistic integrity, detract from her seriousness. But she did Pepsi. Why? She made the rules. She is not viewed drinking the stuff. The closest she gets is to be seen twice holding a can of Pepsi. It was a disaster for Pepsi, but Madonna got her money and forests of publicity. And did the people she offend buy records anyway?

So, did Madonna indulge in a corporate ambush? Robert Mosconi was then the senior creative director at BBDO World-wide Advertising. He worked closely with Madonna on the commercial and remembers:

One day Madonna, who liked to joke with me, came up and said: 'Hey, Robert, are you going to have the burning cross reflecting in the Pepsi can?' And I said: 'What burning cross?' And she smiled and said: 'You'll see.'

Asked the secret of her success, Madonna put forward her considered theory: 'It comes from a rebelliousness and desire to fuck with people.'

Up on the hill with her faxes and her mighty Merlin phone lines, this empress of often carnal commerce agreed to talk to the shoemaker, Niké. Madonna was to endorse a new dance shoe. The fee would be $4.25 million. The negotiations went on in the Hollywood Hills, but a Niké executive (sworn to secrecy) said that quite literally the stumbling block was that Madonna wanted to keep her endorsement and enthusiasm at a minimum: 'She wouldn't even put the damn shoes on her feet!' The deal seemed to be off. Madonna could not – nudge, nudge – understand why. She called Philip Knight, the chairman of Niké. She called and called and called. Then, her lawyers called, threatening to sue for the $4.25 million even though no commercial was filmed. It ended in a stand-off. If we ignore the enjoyment Madonna gets from 'fucking with people'.

While she was being the hard-headed businesswoman, the supposed 'tyrant', it ironically turned out that *Like a Prayer* was Madonna's most personal work. Critics called it 'honest'. It was certainly effective. In 'Keeping It Together', she sings, 'I hit the big time but I still get the blues.' In 'Till Death Do Us Part', she recalls marriage: 'The bruises they will fade away/You hit so hard with the things you say/He takes a drink, she goes inside/He starts to scream, the vases fly/He wishes that she wouldn't cry/He's not in love with her anymore.' On 'Promise to Try', a little girl – 'her face frozen in time' – is comforted by her mother. 'Oh Father' is the freedom from a strict father: 'Maybe someday when I look back I'll be able to say you didn't mean to be cruel/Somebody hurt you too.' And there was the up-tempo 'Express Yourself' which was to become her seventeenth music video. It was a thumb in the nose at the good taste brigade who had jumped on her 'Like a Prayer'. It was called a carnal mini-movie all about making love not money. She was in black – stockings, suspenders and corset – and rolling her stomach, grabbing her crotch and seen chained to a bed lapping at a saucer of milk. It was, she would admit, a grand fuck-you to those who had tried to control her.

Madonna was, and is, a magnet for controversy. Pop queen Debbie Gibson piped up saying she was concerned about how ten-year-olds would accept the latest videos. Madonna herself stuck it to LaToya Jackson saying a *Playboy* layout done by Michael's sister was a sign of 'desperation' and bitching: 'She must have had a major breast job done.' It was even more fun for Madonna when

LaToya answered back: 'Madonna is not a lady, never has been and never will be.' Her breasts? 'If I'd had them done, they'd have looked a lot better than they did in *Playboy*.'

At the top of the hill, it was fun. If a little lonely. Madonna was linked to many men, but there were none. The only regular overnighter was her brother Christopher of whom she says:

Christopher's gay, and he and I have always been the closest members of my family. It's funny. When he was really young, he was so beautiful and had girls all over him, more than any of my other brothers. I knew something was different, but it was not clear to me. He was like a girl magnet. They all seemed incredibly fond of him and close to him in a way I hadn't seen men with women.

I'll tell you when I knew. After I met Christopher [Flynn], I brought my brother to my ballet class because he wanted to start studying dance. I just saw something between them. I can't even tell you exactly what. But then I thought, *Oh, I get it. Oh, OK. He likes men too.* It was an incredible revelation, but I didn't say anything to my brother yet. I'm not even sure he knew. He's two years younger than me. He was still a baby. I could just feel something.

She talked of her family's reaction:

My father's very old-fashioned, traditional, grew up in that macho Italian world. I know he's probably not really comfortable with it. He doesn't treat my brother any differently than all of us, but I know that there's an unspoken thing where Christopher doesn't feel like he's accepted by my father. All of my other brothers and sisters certainly accept it. God knows what my father accepts in my life, you know what I mean? My father is a very silent man. He keeps a lot inside.

The only others staying over were business people sleeping in the spare room. Madonna paid for the best help. She is America's biggest-earning female performer; her income is more uplifting than even the most notorious of her black bras. Since 1986 – and if she is coy about any figures it is her financial ones – she has earned around $197 million. Before tax. She is the boss, the president of a corporation that employs hundreds ('I keep Warner Brothers in work!') and going nowhere but into more profit. For the Time Warner Corporation, she has sold more than half a billion dollars' worth of records – as well as the hundreds of millions more for those involved in the concerts and videos and all manner of other spin-offs.

And she is involved in every deal. Her lawyers and accountants are there to advise her, to tell her what to do. In return, they do well. Freddy DeMann, as her personal manager, makes ten per cent of her earnings; her lawyer, Paul Schindler of Grubman, Indursky and Schindler of New York, is regarded as a top professional and gets five per cent, as does business manager Bert Pedall. But there are contract clauses which keep these advisers within the one to two million dollars a year range – each. A tour manager gets ten per cent of the box-office – it could in fact cost her money to tour given her elaborate productions and narrow profit margin.

Madonna knew for a long time that the way to make money in Hollywood was the movies. But only the right movies. David Geffen, who is one of America's wealthiest men from his record-production companies, real estate and other investments, has been a long-time friend and adviser to Madonna. They have both been active in AIDS charities, but in more than grandstand fund-raising. Homosexuals were Madonna's first fans and she has never deserted them. Her *Bloodhounds of Broadway* director, Howard Brookner, was desperately ill in St Vincent's Hospital in New York where Madonna would make regular visits. Brookner's friend, Brad Gooch, recalls: 'She was incredibly supportive – she not only visited him, but all the other patients in the AIDS ward. It was like Judy Garland visiting another sort of Oz.' Madonna wanted the Hollywood end of the rainbow.

It was David Geffen who sent Madonna to a psychiatrist to deal with her emotions over her mother's death and her father's remarriage. He also sent her to Warren Beatty. He told her to call the legendary Hollywood bedhopper, the man who is a legend in his own bedtime, the man who could make her a movie star just like Marilyn. Warren Beatty was limping away from the financial and critical flop, *Ishtar*, and working on a long-time project for a big screen workout as *Dick Tracy*.

Madonna got her role as Breathless Mahoney. And many

prattled on about how she was working for actors' scale – the minimum wage – of $1440 a week. What was not revealed was Madonna's business negotiations which are now part of privileged Hollywood history, especially at Jeffrey Katzenberg's frugal Disney Studios. She would, in return for her services, receive 'points', a good share of all gross box-office takings – and video and merchandising sales. A casual estimate would put that around $7 million – more than Meryl Streep makes for three movies. And, of course, there would be the $14 million from the *Dick Tracy* soundtrack album. And the Blonde Ambition Tour – America's Home Box Office cable-television station paid $1 million to screen just one concert – and other spin-offs.

Madonna has an excellent sense of sell. But how was she going to cope with get-your-pants-down-as-fast-as-possible Mr Warren Beatty?

FOURTEEN

BREATHLESS

'I think seventy-five per cent of the country wants Warren Beatty's approval. Oh, probably seventy-five per cent have had him.'

MADONNA IN 1990

She called him 'Old Man'. He called her 'Buzzbomb'. Everyone else called them the Odd Couple. Beatty was a challenge to Madonna. But she also saw him as a serious possibility for happiness. He had a history. He would not be intimidated. He was cool. He was also fifty-two when they started work on *Dick Tracy*. Beatty, the first male sex symbol of the sixties, had been toying with the idea of the film since 1975 and the days of Julie Christie and *Shampoo*. After an early meeting with Madonna about her playing Breathless Mahoney, the couple and five others involved in the film went for lunch at the Columbia Bar and Grill, a Tinseltown hangout at the corner of Sunset Boulevard and Gower. South on Gower is the 'technical' Hollywood, the sound studios and the editing rooms. It is where Beatty is happiest.

MADONNA

Inside the Columbia, the Beatty table talked over Perrier and salads with lemon-juice dressing. It was time to go. Beatty asked if he could open an account and the young waitress asked: 'Who are you?' Madonna said: 'See, Old Man,' and paid for lunch. It was a lesson in the demographics of youth and quickly learned.

'I'd seen Madonna as a very good possibility for the movie early on,' Beatty told me as we talked at his work studio on Gower. But he explained:

She was not cast when we were working on the script, but it's peculiar – you write a character and then you cast a character and wonder how anyone else could have possibly played it. And you could have been turned down by fifteen people.

You can see Beatty's instant attraction for Madonna, and it has got nothing to do with bed. It is to do with work, with Hollywood, with the movies. Beatty can drop names as well as his pants. Madonna, the impatient anxious to learn Madonna, wanted to hear everything. We were talking about him casting Madonna as Breathless and it brought on other thoughts:

When I first met Faye Dunaway, I was very impressed with her. I thought she was going to be a very important actress, but I didn't think she was right for Bonnie. I introduced her to Arthur [Penn] who was directing, and he immediately saw her in the part. Eventually, I could. Can you imagine anyone but Michael J. Pollard playing C.W.?

What about Jack Warden in *Shampoo* or *Heaven Can Wait*. Listen, I'll tell you a story. We'd gone to about seven people who turned us down and finally we went to Jack. Jack said yes. About three weeks before we started shooting, he came to me and said he'd found a picture that he'd rather do. He said: 'Of course, I'm going to keep my word to you. I said I'll be in this, and I'll be in it. I just want to appeal to you as a fellow actor, but keep in mind if you say no, the answer is no, and that's fine. I've found this other picture I'd like to do, but if you say no, that's fine. You tell me no, then the answer is no. I'd like to ask you – can I do the other picture?'

I said: 'No.' He said: 'What do you mean, no?' I told him he was going to be very funny in the picture and he did it and he was. We laugh a lot about it now. It wouldn't have been *Shampoo* without him, or *Heaven*. I would have preferred not to have directed *Tracy*. I always prefer not to direct, but usually

I go to a lot of people, and a lot of people turn me down. I didn't ask anybody else to direct *Reds* because I felt there could be problems of vision.

When I originally developed *Heaven Can Wait*, I wanted Muhammad Ali to be the boxer, but he couldn't fit it into his schedule. I cast myself, but I couldn't see myself as a boxer, but I had been a footballer as a kid, so I changed it. I only decided at the last minute to direct it. I had asked Mike [Nichols] and Arthur [Penn], but they were busy.

He finally also brought in Buck Henry to co-star and to co-direct *Heaven Can Wait*. Warren Beatty and his friends and Madonna.

In *Dick Tracy*, he got Michael J. Pollard (as Bugs) and Estelle Parsons (as Tess Trueheart's mom) from *Bonnie and Clyde* and he considers the question of friendship longer than others:

When you've known someone for a long time you begin to see colours and facets in their personality that you just don't see in other people because you don't know them as well. So, when you're writing you think of them. Michael J. I've known for more than thirty years. We did a play together when we were kids. I don't know if it necessarily makes me feel more comfortable. I enjoy it a lot. I see people that I've known for ever. It's just that you fantasize about someone doing something and then they kind of do it. They see what you thought.

If there's a problem you go to someone. That's very much so. Jack [Nicholson], Dustin [Hoffman], Al [Pacino], Diane [Keaton] – these are people whose opinions I value very, very, very highly. They have tremendously fresh insights on something. When you've been editing and seen so much the whole subject becomes goofy. You get someone to come in and sometimes they can help restore your original intentions. They get you to where you were at the beginning.

Madonna was to learn about true inside knowledge from Beatty who explained:

When you know someone a long time, you know their points of orientation. If someone has a very strong social conscience for instance – Julie Christie comes to mind – I would know that showing a piece of work to Julie Christie would be a very strong consideration.

That often happens on a set when you direct. Sometimes I think that when an actor directs, he is not really directing he is just pretending to direct – what he is really doing is listening to the opinions and sensing the opinions of people around him whom he knows and respects as he does his audience. It's very difficult to be your own audience.

Beatty pauses for a long time and then adds:

In fact, it's impossible. I think I try to make the type of movie I want to make and I think that I credit the audience with being at least as sophisticated as I am. Frankly, I worry more about the people who are more sophisticated. Audiences are very hip and brutally honest about things. They're not really worried about your feelings.

Beatty is tall and so are many of the stories about him and that is easy to understand. He is a parcel of vanity and vulnerability, a sort of paranoid Peter Pan. Which is why when you meet him, the mind turns into a flickering film of beautiful images – a gallery of faces from a celebrity concubine revolving for more than thirty years.

Madonna was one of – but not the last – the faces of the nineties. If Garbo talked, well, we all know what Beatty did. And does. And by all accounts, rather well. He is also rather good on the telephone which is his other famous appendage. We all remember Joan Collins on that one: 'Three, four, five times a day was not unusual for him, and he was able to accept phone calls at the same time.' It is a dusty quote and when Madonna was asked on television if she was jealous of Collins, she replied: 'Have you seen her lately?'

'Is Warren satiable?' was the next question. Eyebrow raised, she replied: 'He's satiable.'

Beatty's other passion in life is making movies. He has not made many, but most have been memorable. He was the star, the producer and the director of *Dick Tracy*, which was made for more than $30 million. It was the teaming of a tightly run corporation and indulgent, and usually indulged, film-maker. The result was Beatty's first box-office success in a decade and probably his biggest ever. The film – quite literally a comic strip brought to life in primary colours – is a huge enjoyment.

Beatty has been involved on and off with the project for years. He sort of slouches around the editing room looking more like a university don than a Don Juan. He is 6 ft. 2 in. with curly, slightly thinning hair which he is scratching, and you can see the pitter patter of crows' feet around those bedroom eyes. At one point, he took off his Oliver People's glasses and rubbed them. He had a full cup of coffee in his hand and swirled it around. For the next two hours, he would never drink from the cup. It was his prop. 'Am I a perfectionist? The positive way of saying it is that you are a professionalist. The negative way is to say you're an obsessive. The humorous way is to say you are anal retentive.'

Jeffrey Katzenberg says he had more late nights during the production of *Dick Tracy* than in his entire life because of – Warren Beatty.

I've spent more time on the phone than I ever thought possible. It used to be that my phone conversations lasted ten minutes, but now they can go on for hours. Warren requires an enormous amount of time and support and input. He is totally collaborative. I have never *ever* been asked so many questions by a film-maker. I don't want to make this sound self-important. Warren asked me a thousand questions a day, but I believe he also asked another thousand people those same questions.

The *Dick Tracy* deal took a lot of doing. The ghosts of the $40-million-bomb, *Ishtar*, and the critical, but not commercial, success of the $35 million *Reds* hovered around the negotiating table. Katzenberg revealed the background to what was to be Madonna's 'breakthrough' movie:

We created a situation for Warren in which he was enormously rewarded for remaining disciplined to his own concept of how he was going to make the movie. I've got to give him 101 per cent credit. The corridors were there but the fact is he didn't bump against the walls very often.

We must have spent two years negotiating this deal with Warren. Warren is at his best at ten, eleven at night when I'm at my worst. I think Warren wanted to prove to himself – and maybe to the rest of the world, but mostly to himself – that he could take the responsibility and bring the movie in for a price.

And what Disney got was Beatty's vision of the Chester Gould comic strip which began life in the *Detroit Mirror* in 1931. By the fifties 'Dick Tracy' had sixty-five million readers in 550 newspapers nationwide. Gould created a rogue's gallery of wonderful villains and several of them came to life through the wizardry of prosthetics. There was the story that Beatty had offered President Reagan the role of Pruneface. True? Beatty laughs. 'No – but I'd have grabbed him if I could. I would have been very happy to get him.'

He did get Madonna whose 1990 album, *Madonna: I'm Breath-less* – as well as two other spin-offs – were 'inspired' by the film. The records were part of the behemoth marketing animal which Disney hoped would roar on and on. (Merchandising from *Dick Tracy* handcuffs, key rings and fingerprint sets to vinyl dolls of Breathless and Tracy, and coffee-mugs-on-wheels were wrongly anticipated as at least rivalling 1989's Batmania.)

Beatty was the man who got up every morning and looked in the bathroom mirror and said: '*I'm* with Madonna.' They were as likely a couple as the sexy Bonnie and the sexually confused Clyde. Or the self-important McCabe and manipulative Mrs Miller. But Beatty was smitten. Madonna joined a long breakfast list that includes Joan Collins, Natalie Wood, Leslie Caron, Michelle Phillips, Isabelle Adjani, Julie Christie. Long list? Beatty smiles: 'I never talk about anything to do with personal relationships in my life. I never have. I don't ever intend to. If you ever see me quoted on the subject, you'll know that someone was making it up.'

Ah, the Warren Beatty legend?

These are important people to me. I don't want to hurt them by discussing them in public. As for my love life, I can't control what other people say about it; it is what it is. I know that movie actors are overrewarded in our society and that the press has to cut people like me down to size. So they come up with all sorts of wild things. They make me into an insane eccentric with an incredible fear of losing my youth who lives in a bomb shelter, who contemplated or who is going through plastic surgery, who has devastating relationships with women. It goes through cycles. First they say that women like me too much; then women don't like me at all; then they like me too much again. Somewhere along the way they say I secretly like men – but then the men don't like me! I'm old. I'm young. I'm intelligent. I'm stupid. My tide goes in and out.

Madonna has now become what Beatty was in his heyday – an object of overwhelming fascination. What makes such icons tick? Is all the attention water off a superstar's back?

I'd like to say you develop an immunity to it, but I'm afraid it's more like an allergy. The only defence that you have is not to co-operate. The problem is that by not co-operating you give freedom to the media to invent an unlimited amount of crap because they will do it. I have decided it's best probably not to be so circumspect about it. Not that it's likely to. . . . We had a very reactionary Southern Senator who went to the Supreme Court and became a brilliant, articulate Justice. His point of view on free speech was that all libel laws should be eliminated. There should be no recourse. At least the public would know that there is nothing you can do. The problem now is that you have to prove malicious intent and all kinds of nonsense that enables the public to think the things are fifty per cent true.

But if you're a person who believes in free speech, let alone a person who doesn't want to spend their whole life and fortune fighting some sort of legal battle about what is said in the media, you ignore it.

Beatty has never married, but the warmest he would get to that subject is to talk about Dick Tracy: 'He has primary emotions, a man who would really like to have the joys of family but is pulled by duty and doesn't know whether he can live up to the obligations of a family. He's tempted.' On himself: 'I wouldn't mind being married. I'd like to have children.'

So, of course, would Madonna. But there was little hope with Beatty who was born in Richmond, Virginia, where he and his sister, Shirley MacLaine, were brought up by their headmaster father. 'I am close to my family. My father died in 1988 and I talk to my mother every day or couple of days. And my sister and I are in communication with each other. We get along very well.'

He's not too forthcoming on his sister's reincarnation ideas:

I did make a film about it [*Heaven Can Wait*]. It makes me think of the time when my father was dying. I remember him sitting on the side of the bed, his feet were kind of dangling, and he said to me: 'Warren, what do you think about these ideas of Shirley's?' I said: 'I don't know what to think of them.' He said: 'I just don't think I want to do what I have to do to find out.'

His father had him reading by the age of four, but as a teenager he gave up the books. He was president of his class, captain of the high-school football team (something he remains proud of), but after a year at university, moved to New York to study acting. He did not want to be 'in anybody else's shadow' – his sister, who is three years older, had by then established herself.

'I wanted to be a stage director – that was legitimate. I wanted to write for the theatre. I sort of backed into acting as a way of learning the theatre.' In late-fifties New York, he worked on stage and on some live television shows. He auditioned for director Josh Logan with another film novice, Jane Fonda. Nothing happened. Three months later, MGM gave him a five-year contract at $400 a week. At twenty-two, he was in Hollywood. He was also quick to catch on. He did not like the look of the studio system, so he borrowed the money to pay off his contract and went back to New York.

There, he managed to win a supporting role in William Inge's play *A Loss of Roses*. The show flopped – Beatty sailed on. Director Elia Kazan saw him on stage and cast him opposite Natalie Wood in *Splendor in the Grass*. Before the film that was to make him an instant sensation even opened, he was a 'star' – in the gossip columns. His public affair with Wood broke up her marriage to Robert Wagner (they later married again) and Peter Hall would later name him in the diector's divorce from Leslie Caron.

And that is the image we have had ever since – the lover boy, the Casanova, the Lothario who cannot keep his hands off women even when they are entangled with someone else. Lee Grant is a veteran of Hollywood and appeared in Beatty's *Shampoo*. She says: Warren's conquests of women are not totally successful. His percentage is about 50-50. Those who he can't conquer, don't want to be part of a crowd – one of Warren's girls. But the Peter Pan quality in Warren is very attractive to some. He teaches them to fly and they have extraordinary experiences with him. Then they grow up and go on and he keeps flying. Like Peter Pan, he always comes back to another little girl who's ready to fly off with him to Never-Never Land.

Madonna? Maybe she can also be in his sequel to *Shampoo*. 'I've never done a sequel. The idea has never appealed to me. But

I'm sort of interested in doing a sequel to *Shampoo*. It's a real good cast.' Such a project would reunite his randy Beverly Hills hairdresser, George, who cavorted with Julie Christie and Goldie Hawn and Carrie Fisher to the backdrop of the 1960 election of Richard Nixon as President. But, we wondered, given today's sexual climate, would the coupling-addicted George still be around today? Beatty gave his warmest smile: 'Oh, I think he would be. If you're saying he was high risk, he's not reality. Oh, I think George would still be with us. Nixon's still with us – that's a higher risk.'

The satirical sexual comedy was much discussed in the seventies. What did this mean? Or that? It became a topic, and in some quarters, an intellectual platform. Beatty says his motives for the film were:

I wanted to explore sexuality through a Don Juan. A Don Juan doesn't get that way out of a misogynist feeling or the idea that he's a latent homosexual who's seducing all these women because he really wants to seduce men, or out of impotence or the desire to degrade women. He just wants to fuck because he likes to fuck.

Would an older George have settled down? Say with a younger woman? Madonna saw a life in that scenario.

FIFTEEN

THE CHARMER

'I'd like to come back as Warren Beatty's fingertips.'

WOODY ALLEN ON REINCARNATION

Madonna quickly fell under the Beatty spell. He is the charmer of Hollywood. But, of course, there were all the women before her. And for all her confidence, it bothered her. Could she ever be as wonderful as Bardot at age twenty-five? Or the late Natalie Wood? Then, with her trademark positive thinking, she would tell herself she was better than any of them. Beatty was protective and a father-figure for her and certainly not easily shocked.

Warren understands the bullshit. He's been an icon for years. He's had a lot more practice at it than I have. Obviously somebody who hasn't experienced it would be more threatened by my fame than he is. You can't understand being hugely famous until it happens and then it's too late to decide if you want it or not. Warren's been a sex symbol for so long, he's just not surprised by anything.

Not by Madonna. Beatty lobbed back:

I don't know that there are many people who can do as many things as Madonna. People who are in a positive frame of mind, who bring as much energy and willingness to work as Madonna does. She has in this respect a real healthy humility about the cinema. I think this is a prime requisite to be able to function in cinema – or, actually, in art. I think she's courageous in the areas she explores artistically. I think that's what she wants to explore. I think her generous spirit would be the thing I think informs her work the most. As she goes on, she will gain the artistic respect that she already deserves. She has an unlimited future as an actress.

Beatty, true to his word, would not talk about the romantic relationship. Madonna talked about their situation: 'Sometimes I'm cynical and pragmatic and think it will last as long as it lasts. Then I have moments when I'm really romantic and I think: We're *just perfect* together.' Of course, she should have remained pragmatic and although it is difficult to imagine Madonna as the victim in a relationship, she was about to become one – for the second time. After the divorce from Penn, she had felt a complete failure. That, in time, was replaced by a deep sadness which – like a good Catholic girl – she still feels today. However, she felt it was like dealing with a death.

Dick Tracy – 'Dead-eyed Dick' as the character and Beatty were known on the film set – was much more fun than her previous film encounters. Madonna was also involved in the music by Stephen Sondheim, the man regarded as the genius of modern musical theatre. The challenge for Madonna was to get the songs over without sounding like Eliza Doolittle. Sondheim remembers her impatience:

She hates to make a lot of choices. For us, she did two and sometimes had to be persuaded to do three takes. It was her dancing that convinced me. I was really knocked out the moment she started to move – that's when you immediately know why she's a star.

Madonna was not sure she could do justice to Sondheim's songs. Everyone else – including Sondheim – was. As buttery-haired *femme fatale*, Breathless Mahoney, she delivered. She was concerned – irked and bothered by the lack of success of *Shanghai*

Surprise, Who's That Girl? and *Bloodhounds of Broadway* – that she should pull off the role. She had turned down *The Fabulous Baker Boys* which won Michelle Pfeiffer an Oscar nomination.

How did she like the film in which Pfeiffer co-starred with Jeff and Beau Bridges? 'I hated it. It was too mushy. Such a Wonder-bread cast. I think of all these people as being Californian people – blonde and boring.' She had also refused Oliver Stone's *Evita* test.

The movies? I'm going to keep trying. *Dick Tracy* will help me a lot. Warren says I'm great in it and I don't think he lies about stuff like that. He's really helpful reading scripts. He has an infinite knowledge about what makes a good movie, a good director. He's a sounding board for me. He's critical and that's good.

Warren should have been a psychiatrist or a district attorney. When he wants to know somebody, he goes out of his way to investigate. You feel like you are under the microscope. You're not used to people spending that much time trying to get to know you. But it's admirable. Everybody ought to examine the people they're going to work for as intensely as he does.

I've been drawn to so many different kinds of men, I couldn't say if I've got a type. Let's say I'm attracted to men who are in touch with their sexuality – who are aware of it and who *work* it. And I prefer men who can acknowledge their feminine side. I think I have a lot of masculinity in me. Macho guys don't really go for me – certainly not when they get to know me. They're frightened of their feminity.

You imbue men with the characteristics you want them to have. Then they're not what you expect at all. But it's your own fault for not doing your homework, the investigating, the finding out. I'm more cautious now, but I'm still a hopeless romantic.

The filming and loving days with Beatty were fun. They were in restaurants all over Los Angeles. Once on a trip to New York they were heading out to Kennedy Airport and the 6:30 p.m flight to California when she leaned over and whispered: 'Let's go to Paris.' The limousine driver told me Beatty did not blink, and simply picked up the car phone and made reservations.

Indulgent away from the film set, the actor-director was still the boss. And a perfectionist. Take after take after take. Al Pacino won a deserved Oscar nomination for his turn as loony bad-guy Big Boy Caprice, who is after Dick Tracy. In one sensational sequence he shows his chorus line, including Madonna, how to strut their stuff. Madonna remembers too well co-starring with one perfectionist in front of the camera and being directed by another behind it:

As Big Boy, he was always smacking my butt and my face. I hated him, I loathed him. He'd tell me the dirtiest jokes, suck on his cigar like it was some sort of weird phallic symbol and just be a pig. So off-camera, I'd always move away from him but he'd always grab me and go: 'Get over here.' This is exactly what happens in the movie. . . . He made me cry sometimes. There was a scene where Al kept smacking me in the stomach. It would sting and what made me cry was not so much the hit, but that Warren wouldn't shout 'Cut'. Al just kept going and I was humiliated. And of course that was what they intended – they wanted me to show the right emotion as Breathless.

Madonna plotted revenge on Pacino, who was shy with her when they were not filming. As they rehearsed the big dance scene in which she wore a fur coat, she suddenly dropped the fake fur to the floor revealing she was naked. Pacino blushed. He didn't know where to look and only got the joke when Madonna's co-prankster Beatty burst into laughter. In another scene, Madonna walks into a room, takes off her jacket and runs her hands down her sides. It took a number of takes. Perfectionist? Anal retentive?

Away from work, they were at the Catch One disco, a predomi-nantly black-gay club where a scene from the film *Beaches* was shot. Or eating at the Columbia Grill or the Great Greek and on to the funky Club Louis. 'They were at all the parties – they were everywhere,' remembers Lonny Roland, a Club Louis regular. They were also at Adriano's just off Mulholland up in the hills or at the popular Citrus restaurant on Hollywood's ever-so-trendy Melrose Avenue. At most places, Madonna would finally find her way on to Beatty's lap.

Madonna and Sandra Bernhard remained great friends. They still had their 'gang'. As Penn was a member of the Brat Pack, the girls called themselves the 'Snatch Batch'. If she wasn't with Beatty she was with the 'Batch'.

On the David Letterman Show, Bernhard for a joke confessed to having slept with both Sean and Madonna. And Madonna said the two of them hung out in a Greenwich Village lesbian bar known as the Cubby Hole.

I've never been to the Cubby Hole. That's the joke of it. My brother Christopher lived around the corner and I've walked by it with him and I'd sort of go, 'Oh, yeah, look, there's a lesbian club.' Sandra and I were just 'fucking' with people. But then when I realized the reaction we had gotten, I, of course, couldn't leave that alone. So Sandra and I decided to tease everybody. Then, of course, it got out hand and I didn't want to do it anymore, because it was more important for me to have a friendship. But we had our fun with that and it sort of worked itself to death.

What about, say, her supposed relationship with Jennifer Grey? 'That came out of me and Sandra Bernhard. Then it became a question of whatever female I had a close relationship with who is an outspoken girl – which Jennifer is – then I must be sleeping with her.'

A waitress at Odeon, a restaurant in New York, remembers a night when Madonna and Jennifer and five other women came in for a late-night supper.

Madonna ordered a house salad and everybody else ordered a house salad. She said she didn't want dressing on it – or cheese. The others – except for Jennifer Grey who was bold enough to order cheese – said they didn't want them either. When the salads came, Madonna ate hers with her fingers; all the others ate theirs with their fingers too. Weird. And she kept looking at me. Maybe she just liked my outfit, but she was so obvious about it. Like it was a dare. Or *something*.

The hopes or fantasies or both of a New York waitress were far from Madonna's thoughts. She and Beatty were on the rounds. She celebrated her thirty-first birthday with him at actor Mickey Rourke's Rubber Club. She was also working and creating. Her Siren Films was making plans to film Frida Kahlo's life story –

doing for the Mexican artist what Beatty had done for radical writer John Reid in his Oscar-winning film, *Reds*. Then there were the songs for *Madonna: I'm Breathless*. Sondheim penned his three but Madonna believed hers were 'the real shit'. They included 'Hanky Panky' which tells of the pleasures of being bound and spanked on the bottom.

Madonna got the Bad Taste Attention Award again and rubbed it in by going on the Arsenio Hall talk-show to say how much she likes to receive an erotic spanking. Taste? There was also the song 'Now I'm Following You' with the line: 'Dick . . . that's an interesting name/My bottom hurts just thinking about you.' It was Stephen Sondheim who collected the Best Original Song Oscar for his 'Sooner or Later (I Always Get My Man)', provocatively performed by Madonna at the 1991 Academy Awards at the Shrine Auditorium in Los Angeles.

But the Oscars were still just a possibility when Beatty and Madonna slipped – forty minutes late which is early for Beatty – into a Hollywood screening room to see a rough-cut of Sandra Bernhard's film, *Without You I'm Nothing*. In the film of her stage performance, Bernhard imagines a sex session with Beatty and tells him to put on two condoms: 'Oh, baby it's no reflection on how much I care about you. We all know you've been around.' Beatty and Madonna – in his lap – laughed together.

And in 1990 *Dick Tracy* was being filmed. Costume designer Milena Canonero wanted Madonna's Breathless to represent the night, the moon and sex. He put her into midnight blue, silver and black. And that was *tight* midnight-blue, silver and black dresses. They flashily displayed Madonna's every exercised curve – one dress was cut so low, she literally fell out of it during rehearsals. Watching, Beatty smiled: 'She's dressed in a way that accentuates her good health.'

Which was very much in. And needed to be in. Madonna suggested she could promote *Dick Tracy* with a tour – what was to become the Blonde Ambition Tour.

Disney didn't come to me and ask me to market the movie. Let's just say I was killing twelve birds with one stone. It's a two-way street. . . . Most people didn't associate me with movies, but I knew I have a much bigger following than Warren. A lot of my audience isn't aware of who he is.

The woman who David Geffen calls the 'superstar sex goddess of the video generation' was about to go into action. And to get emotionally hurt again.

SIXTEEN

MADONNA INC.

'*As easy as it would be for me to nail a custard pie to the wall.*'

SHIRLEY MACLAINE IN 1991 ON HOW EASILY SHE COULD COPE WITH MADONNA AS A SISTER-IN-LAW

Madonna Incorporated is a smooth-running machine, just like the boss of the company. She has surrounded herself with experts – in everything from music through hair-dressing to stage construction. And what links them all is the Madonna Secrets Act which works exactly like the British Government's Official Secrets Act. Those who join the Firm do not talk on the record. Even platitudes. Usually. All the team work on the Madonna image, but such is the confidence in the product that they have now opened up about how they get that package ready for the road.

In just a few years, Madonna has been so many different people – the Material Girl of 1985, all Marilyn in hot pink and strapless gowns; she was one of the boys in 1986 with chopped hair and black cap and her 'Open Your Heart'; in 1989 it was the adrogynous look, the man's suit and no shirt; *Like a Prayer* was black lingerie and a cross and chain; by 1991 she was Marilyn Monroe incarnate bumping and grinding at the Oscars and belting out 'Sooner or Later'. That night, the talk dwelled not on Kevin Costner's Oscar wins for *Dances with Wolves*, but on Madonna and her extravaganza appearance with Michael Jackson. They were a couple setting down to business. The other top topic was Madonna's figure. It was the one she got for the Blonde Ambition Tour. And you don't just wake up looking like that.

Madonna's secret is Robert Parr, a former baseball player with a crooked grin and a degree in exercise physiology. She recruited him to the Team in 1987, and although he also works with Theresa Russell and Tatum O'Neal and, in 1991, O'Neal's husband John McEnroe, his number-one client and advertisement for his California-based 'Up To Parr' personal-trainer business is Madonna.

Theresa Russell says:

Madonna is a friend of mine. She eats, breathes, and sleeps everything in her career. It must catch up with her, even though I think she realizes it too in a way. I don't know what she is going to do. When I compared myself with her, I used to think how lazy I was, and then I realized how much I prefer my life.

Parr is, of course, more positive.

She challenges herself more than I ever could. Our workouts often start at five in the morning when she is filming. We work on stamina and endurance for her singing and dancing and we work on the shape of her body. This transformation is not an overnight thing. Madonna realizes how important her health and fitness are to her performances. She knows how she wants to look and she works hard at it.

Our workouts are very focused. Doing different combinations of exercise is what creates muscle balance and avoids injuries by building up overall strength. The cardiovascular training also helps Madonna's singing by enabling her to achieve a more efficient use of oxygen. We wanted to incorporate the sinewy look. We wanted strength and endurance instead of mass and power. The advantages of working out are not only physical, they are mental. We go running or biking and then she does thirty minutes on the

Lifecycle or Versaclimber – it simulates mountain climbing with the legs and arms in motion. We cool down by running stairs. Madonna then works out with ten- and twenty-pound weights. Her upper-body definition comes from weight repetitions, the flat stomach is from a combination of sit-ups and pike-position lifts that work the upper, lower and oblique abdominal muscles.

The sinewy look is created with workouts and also with low body fat. Madonna is a vegetarian, and she travels with a vegetarian cook. And she drinks gallons of water to replace lost body fluids. My biggest problem is making sure she has enough complex carbohydrates and protein so she doesn't get too thin because of her workouts and her performances. We finish the workout with fifteen minutes of stretching – first the large muscle groups and then the smaller upper-body muscles.

Madonna has the genetic potential to achieve what she has and she truly enjoys challenging herself. Not everyone could look like her, but with the right, intelligent workout, everyone can look better. But it takes time and dedication to build the endurance and stamina to then create muscle tone and shape.

You change the routine for the look. Warren Beatty wanted a softer-in-the-shoulder look for *Dick Tracy*, and we did that. Then you change the intensity level a little.

When we're on tour, I go out about 6 a.m. and find a running course, a mix of flat and hills close to where we're staying. Then we'll run up and down the hotel stairs. I'm kinda her sounding board while we run.

Former British commando Tony Toms joined the European leg of the Blonde Ambition Tour in the summer of 1990. By now, Madonna's exercise regimen had taken control of her – she was addicted to it. Onlookers were sent flying as she and her entourage ran through London's Hyde Park. But it wasn't just them who were getting battered – so was Madonna's image. But she could not stop running. Toms reported:

She works harder than an Olympic athlete. It was frightening to see just how fit and strong she is. She had to get rid of some minders because they couldn't keep up with her. The security people think it is just a minding job until they have to go out running with her. It's then they find they can't stand the pace. We were all as fit as fiddles, but working with her still tired us out. We were knackered at the end of the tour. She is just a complete perfectionist over everything, and that includes her figure.

But it is not just vanity. A Madonna concert lasts two hours and she belts out the songs non-stop while dancing around the stage. So she certainly has to be super-fit. Everything and everybody has got to be perfect for a Madonna concert. She will not put up with any slacking. If someone does something wrong, she bawls them out. But equally, she is a kind and caring person. In Barcelona, during 1990's sweltering 100 degree fahrenheit summer, her hairdresser broke her leg in a nasty fall. Madonna was full of concern for the young girl, often bringing her presents to the hospital and sitting by her bedside. She didn't have to. The girl could have been easily replaced, but Madonna isn't like that.

She's also funny. I was at the front of a group of minders surrounding Madonna and trying to push her through 6500 fans at a stadium in Barcelona. She was directly behind me hanging on to my trousers when the belt snapped and they fell down. I had nothing on underneath. But Madonna leaned forward and said sweetly: 'Tony you're supposed to hit 'em, not fuck 'em.'

Australian Peter Chaplin looks after the inside of Madonna's body. He feeds her 'performance food'. Chaplin prepares a high-energy vegetarian diet and says:

Madonna is a professional and takes her fitness training and her diet very, very seriously. To keep her vegetable-fat level up, I feed her lots of avocados. I also make her drink fresh-squeezed fruit juice because the vitamins in the juice are readily absorbed. On one tour I thought up the ideal dish for her – Athletes' Answer. It's pasta with herb sauce and nuts and seeds – real training food.

On concert days, Madonna has dinner at 4:15 p.m. and I try to include recipes that give a complete protein and carbohydrate base to help her cope.

She's very up front and honest. You know where you are with her. If she doesn't like something, she'll tell you.

She likes Chaplin's food. Here are three of her favourites, each of which serves up to four people:

FITNESS NOODLES

Pick your favourite noodles for this dish. The best are 10–12 oz. plain noodles. Cook them according to package directions. Be sure to keep the noodles warm while making the vegetables.

Heat 4 tbls. of vegetable oil in a large frying pan. Add 1 lb. mixed fresh vegetables (such as carrots, celery and red peppers) cut into matchstick-thin strips.

Then add 4 tsp. of crushed garlic. 1 tsp. freshly ground black pepper and 5 oz. unsalted cashew nuts. Stir rapidly for two minutes. Place 4 tbls. soy sauce in a measuring cup and fill with water up to 9 oz. Add to vegetable stir-fry ingredients. Mix well, add drained noodles. Garnish with chives or carrot strips.

AEROBIC APRICOT CURRY

In large frying pan, cook 1 diced onion in 1 tbls. oil. Add 2 diced carrots and 1 diced parsnip. Add 1½ tbls. curry powder, stir 1 min. Or try Madonna's favourite spice mix: tiny amounts of lemongrass, chilli, fenugreek, coriander, five-spice powder, brown and yellow mustard seeds, caraway and ginger.

Add 2 large chopped tomatoes, a few matchstick-thin slices of ginger and natural juice from a 15 oz. can of apricots. Simmer 10 min., add apricots, simmer 10 min. Thicken with a little cornstarch mixed in cold water. Garnish with fresh coriander, lemon juice and tofu cubes cooked in a small amount of curry paste.

ATHLETE'S ANSWER

On baking sheet mix 5 oz. each sunflower and pumpkin seeds and 2½ oz. unsalted peanuts. Bake in 325°F oven 15 min. Mix again, back in oven 10 min. Remove, add dash soy sauce, set aside. In saucepan, boil 4 oz. potatoes. Drain, rinse, set aside. In large pot, boil 12 oz. bow tie pasta 10 min. Heat 1 tbls. olive oil in small pan and saute potatoes 3–4 min. Add 2 tbls. supermarket pesto sauce and 2 tbls. bouillon cube vegetable stock. Drain pasta, toss in 1 tbls. olive oil, return to pot. Add potato mixture. Mix well. Stir in nuts and seeds. Garnish with basil.

Madonna is careful with her body – and outrageous about what she dresses it in. Her favourite designers are Jean-Paul Gaultier and Franco Moschino because she enjoys their sense of humour:
I like to cross the boundaries between men and women. That can be

frightening, but the things I'm most affected by are things that frighten or challenge me. I like to nudge people, to break through stereotypes. There are too many stereotypes. Even liberated women stay in certain categories – no one is too threatening.

She is not easy to work with. Or for. Hairstylist Victor Vidal says:

She knows she's difficult, but her saving grace is that being difficult is part of being honest, for her. She complains for a reason. It might be after fourteen hours of rehearsal and she'll say: 'Let's get this done.'

Vidal bleached, chopped and cropped Madonna for her *True Blue* video:

I told her about this vision I had of her. I wanted her to bleach her hair almost white and cut it short. She thought for a moment and then said yes, picked up a magazine and never looked up until I was finished.

Francesca Tolot and Joanne Gair from Hollywood's popular (with the stars) Cloutier Agency do her professional make-up. There are only two basic rules: use deeper shades of colour when her hair is dark, paler shades when she is blonde. 'She's aware of her face – *she* knows what looks good and what does not,' says Gair in a rare remark. The Cloutier Agency have signed the Madonna Official Secrets Act *en masse*.

Photographer Herb Ritts met Madonna in 1985 when she marched into his studio dripping in rubber bracelets, crucifixes and other trinkets. 'Her attraction isn't about her hair or make-up or clothes, it's about her evolution as a person.' Or as a celebrity chameleon?

For the Blonde Ambition Tour, the plan was for Busby Berkeley to meet Anthony Burgess' *Clockwork Orange*, with costuming by naughty Frederick's of Hollywood. The world was going to 'Vogue': 'I know a place where you can get away, it's called a dance floor/It makes no difference if you're black or white, a boy or a girl.'

What *does* make a difference is Madonna. She has transcended all the rules of entertainment. It is that old chestnut about the telephone book – if she went on stage and read it, people would pay to see her. It is her. It is the Celebrity. Did anybody ever hear the music at a Beatles concert? We went to *see* Elvis, to see Michael Jackson; the Celebrity had overtaken the performer. And that was so clear by the time Madonna strutted out on stage in conical bras and sci-fi bustiers on the Blonde Ambition Tour. High Style. High camp. Electric red lips. Dark eyebrows, the fountain of fake-blonde ponytail. Costumes by Gaultier and her long-time friend Marlene Stewart. Coiffed hair. Plunging necklines. Old Hollywood. Neon Las Vegas. And the corset with the pointy – back in fashion – heavily stitched bra. They went to hear her sing? Getouttahere! Madonna – number one with a bullet bra.

The latest incarnation of Madonna, a twenty-first-century sex siren, a Barbarella, sent Madonna into the nineties. She had messed with every taboo in the eighties from sex and sacrilege to cross-dressing and crucifixes so let's get going. Mimed masturbation? Yes, with 'Like a Virgin'. And there were the topless chaps and their foot-long pointy brassieres. A touch of discipline with 'Hanky Panky' and Madonna chiding: 'You may not know the song, but you all know the pleasures of a good spanking.'

'She said: "Let's break every rule we can." She wanted to make statements about sexuality, cross-sexuality, the church and the like,' recalls Blonde Ambition choreographer Vince Paterson, enthusiastically going on: 'The biggest thing we tried to do was change the shape of concerts. Instead of just presenting songs we wanted to combine fashion, Broadway, rock and performance art.'

A snappy, irreverent mongrel of a show. Paterson remembers an early conversation with Madonna: 'Are you the one who had Michael Jackson grab his balls in the *Bad* video?' she asked.

'No,' said Paterson, 'he was grabbing his balls before I got on the *Bad* video.'

'Well, maybe I should do it,' said Madonna.

'Well, you should, because you have more balls than most of the men I know,' Paterson says he told her.

The tour began in the spring of 1990 in Japan. Everyone learned from the first moment who was in charge. A sound check was being taken in Tokyo and Madonna decided on a certain volume level. A technician questioned her decision and she made it clear: 'Listen. Everyone is entitled to *my* opinion.'

The Blonde Ambition Tour was all part of the Madonna masterplan. She now knew she had to be pragmatic about Beatty. The closest he was to her at present was the seven show dancers in their yellow *Dick Tracy* overcoats and very non-Dick G-strings. Beatty's fingerprints were elsewhere. Madonna was also enjoying a quiet, comfortable love affair. Workers on the tour say she was happy and content. There were only hints to the identity of her lover during the four-month Blonde Ambition Tour.

'*Genki Desu ka?*' shouted Madonna from the scaffolding of the Marine Stadium in Chiba as her tour of Japan began. 'How ya doin?' she followed up with as she started her tour and simultaneously baptized the outdoor stadium which is also the site of Tokyo's Disneyland. There was nothing Mickey Mouse about this enterprise.

After three weeks in Japan, the tour moved to America, eighteen songs in ninety minutes of sell-out controversy. Jean-Paul Gaultier maintains he took 350 aspirins to prepare the costumes for 'the Madonna'. One costume was a beaded acid-green body suit – something Cyd Charisse would have sparkled Fred Astaire with – and Gaultier said he was advised by a *Folies-Bergére* dresser to wash it in a 'non-aggressive detergent'.

In Canada, there was a problem. Police were called to the Skydome Stadium by parents conplaining about Madonna simulating masturbation in 'Like a Virgin' while lying on a red-velvet, gold-brocade bed tilted toward the audience. 'Morality was never involved and there was no prosecution,' say the Toronto Mounties. They did admit that following complaints that the show was lewd, they had agents watch it through binoculars. There is a lot of dedication involved when you always get your man.

Dick Tracy was going into cinemas with great fanfare. And the publicity machine was still trying to push the Madonna/Warren Beatty romance. But this was one man, as Shirley MacLaine told me, that Madonna was not going to hang on to. Beatty does not want to change. At fifty-three he is happily in control of his life. There is Jack and Dustin and Diane and all the others he can speed-dial on his touch-tone phone when he wants company. Madonna, the self-admitted 'hopeless romantic', thought she could change him. When you have succeeded at everything else it must have seemed a safe shot.

But Beatty was Beatty. He spent nights with other women. He made elaborate excuses. Madonna wanted a commitment. So did the world's media. She hit back at Beatty and bombarded Jellybean Benitez with calls. He was staying at a West Hollywood hotel, but before midnight, he was up in the Hollywood Hills to spend the night with Madonna.

She is friendly with Beatty now. She sat on his lap at Swifty Lazar's party at Spago after the 1991 Oscars. But she remains hurt. She is angry that she can not control her men. Her father's actions. Sean Penn's. Warren Beatty's. She can not take control. She does not want wimps, but she can not ride herd on the ones she does want.

It's really a hard thing to accept in life that no matter what you do you can't change a person. If you say: 'I don't want you looking at that woman,' they're going to do it anyway. It doesn't matter what you say. You want to think that if this person is in love with you, you have control over them. But you don't. And to accept that in life is next to impossible. Then again, I want to be a fly on the wall for all Warren Beatty's conversations, but I don't want the reverse.

I'd go: 'Warren, did you really chase that girl for a year?' and he'd say: 'Nay, it's all lies.' I should have known better. I was unrealistic, but then you always think you're going to be the one.

SEVENTEEN

LEATHER AND LACE

'You can have all the success in the world and if you don't have someone to love, it's certainly not as rewarding. The fulfilment you get from another human being – a child in particular – will always dwarf people recognizing you in the street.'

MADONNA IN 1991

If a week is a long time in politics, it can be an eternity in the world of entertainment. Audiences, especially Madonna's video generation of fans, want instant gratification. And, as the joke goes, they want it *now*. Madonna was seeing her psychiatrist two or three times a week. She seemed to have everything – and nothing. She likes everything neat like her closets: she is a symbol of the Filofax generation, her appointments and even her telephone calls are scheduled. She knows it is close to an obsession, like her exercise routine, and that there is a Catch-22. She exercises to stop being depressed and if she did not exercise she would be depressed about not exercising. She does not sleep much. In the early hours she will make lists, plan ahead.

She has taken three holidays in the past ten years and was bored by the second day of each of them. She admits if she had slowed down more she might have held her marriage together and her relationship with Beatty. Interestingly, it is Penn, who in 1991 wrote and directed Charles Bronson in the film, *Indian Runner*, who can now pinpoint Madonna as a woman of today. The traditional role of the male in society is being openly questioned and the new men's movement has grown out of – because of or in reaction to – women's liberation. Penn, a man of the Marlboro-image of masculinity, appears to have mellowed in his view and accepted that women too can have 'balls'. His film debuted well at the Cannes Film Festival in 1991 when Madonna was also promoting her *Truth or Dare* (they even shared the same hotel if not a room) and it is about a returning Vietnam vet trying to start a normal life in the American Midwest.

The film is the story of an American male's struggle. In America today there is no specific place for masculinity. There is no need to go out and hunt for food or kill the guy from the other tribe. But we've hung on to that concept and almost every guy in the US has some need to live up to that tribal rite. There is nothing of value that men can do that women can't so we are in a period of transition – trying to accept what has happened. This movie is about issues that I am trying to work out in my own life. A mature life requires responsibility and that means cutting your losses, the art of compromise.

Sean Penn on the art of compromise: certainly something completely different. Madonna never would:

When I lived with Sean, he loved to ball up his clothes. I'd say: 'You twisted a Versace suit into a ball and *I can't bear it.*' I would follow him and take his things and hang them up. He'd say: 'Leave me alone. I want to do it this way.' But I just couldn't stand it.

Freddy DeMann says of his number-one client: 'Madonna is the biggest star in the universe. And she likes the view.' She admits she is subborn:

I'm the boss. Quite frankly, a lot of things I've wanted have met with adversity. There's always this preliminary shit that's thrown and then there's my shit fit and then I do what I have to do. And they like it.

Dead-Eyed Dick was over. So was the Blonde Ambition Tour. Madonna wanted to make music. She was releasing *The Immaculate Collection*, a best-of compilation of eleven hits and two new songs, 'Rescue Me' and 'Justify My Love'. Madonna went to Paris to film a video to accompany the release of 'Justify My Love'. While she was there she visited the 1990 fashion shows and dismayed the world's fashion editors by sitting opposite them without wearing knickers. They found it a little distracting.

Herb Ritts was there taking pictures. At Thierry Mugler's third show, Madonna sat in the front row wearing a black plastic coat with fake-fur trim and a bare midriff. Two burly minders kept away the photographers. Madonna cheered Lauren Hutton on the catwalk. But she also complained at the fashions: 'Tired, tired – Gaultier's done that.' Diane Brill got the comment: 'She's sooooo fat.' The celebrity crowd got on their feet at the end to give Mugler, arm in arm with Diana Ross, an ovation. Madonna stayed in her seat. Maybe it was to save her energy. She was going to need it, proving that, like her idol Marilyn Monroe's biggest film, 'Some Like It Hot'.

For three days at the Royal Monceau Hotel in Paris, she began to film the video for release of 'Justify My Love'. Appearing with her in it was Tony Ward, a muscled 5 ft. 7 in. tall model with a Roman nose who had been Madonna's 'birthday present' from her brother Mario. Ward, three years younger than Madonna, had done nude modelling and was seen wearing only a smile and an ankle bracelet in Hollywood's gay magazine, *In Touch For Men*. He has also featured in Herb Ritts' book, *Men and Women*. And is known at the Edelweiss night-club in Manhattan, a spot for non-gay businessmen who like to relax by slipping into something comfortable after work – a cocktail dress, wigs and make-up. Jayme Harris, a former girlfriend of Ward, claims he is a keen cross-dresser. She also said he liked whips and chains and was 'quite forward about it'.

Now, he was about to get real exposure. Maybe it was the lesbian kiss. Or the men in fish-net stockings. Or Madonna's all-but-naked bouncing bottom. Or the hints of bisexuality, cross-dressing, group sex, voyeurism, S&M and the full gamut of leather and lace sex. Or Madonna, in her skyscraper heels and scant black lingerie, cavorting with Ward or kissing and nuzzling European model Amanda Cazalet. Or the insinuation of oral sex or the woman in suspenders, her nipples exposed, grasping a man's crotch.

Probably most of that made MTV ban Madonna's *Justify My Love* video. (In Britain the IBA said it could not be shown before 9 p.m.) The video is populated with surreally androgynous performers. There are echoes of Visconti's *The Damned* and Cavani's *The Night Porter*, or the work of the late photographer Robert Mapplethorpe, a controversial tableaux. The message said any fetish was welcome.

But the video was not on MTV. Instead, it became the first video single ever released, selling for $9.98 for five minutes of entertainment. A major hit is around the 50,000 sales mark: 'Justify My Love' was shipped out by the quarter million. In Saudia Arabia black-market copies were selling for $200 a time. Normally performers do not earn from videos – often they pay to make them. Madonna had made other arrangements. She had negotiated a 17.5 per cent share of any sales – before it was even decided to sell the video just in time for Christmas 1990.

But it was the other business that had people talking. Who was kissing Madonna as Ward watched? Amanda Cazalet, seven years younger than Madonna, is employed by the Marilyn Gauthier Modelling Agency in Paris. She is a friend of rock-video mastermind, Jean-Baptise Mondino, who directed the video. 'It was a natural,' said Robert Farrel who is Cazalet's 'booker' at Gauthier, adding: 'Everyone knew that once Madonna met Amanda it was going to be her.' Cazalet would speak only briefly about the video and Madonna: 'After seeing it the first thing you want to do is make love. She knew exactly what she wanted. She had this inner power which is incredible.'

No one at MTV believes that Madonna could have thought they would screen the video. American television has tough double standards. It will titillate to get ratings but it will not challenge the boundaries. The contradictions of 'safe-violence' and 'safe-sex' are what they practise. Standards are like nipples even in Madonna videos. Everyone has two of them.

Madonna went on national American television, on *Nightline*, a heavyweight discussion programme that is broadcast at 11:30 p.m. The show was born during the Iranian hostage crisis and has built an admirable following. With Madonna on the show, the ratings were the second highest in its ten-year history (fallen evangelist Jim Bakker's wife Tammy breaking down live topped Madonna), but she was not in control. At times she was inarticulate. Yet she was as bouncy as Mae West in her heyday. 'You're going to wind up making more money than you would have,' *Nightline*-host Forrest Sawyer told her. She cheekily replied: 'Yeah, so lucky me.'

Of course, as Miss West knew before her, luck had absolutely nothing to do with it. Or goodness. 'She gets as much out of her talent as anyone ever has,' says John Branca, an entertainment lawyer who has represented the Rolling Stones and Michael Jackson. 'Her major assets are controversy and sex appeal and great music.'

As Branca says, controversy is an asset. Even Madonna's garden gets noticed. Her neighbour Donald Robinson went to court arguing that her untrimmed trees ruined his view of Los Angeles. She claimed people were looking into her property. Her brother Christopher, a bodyguard, a gardener and one of her assistants testified for her. She did not go to court because of death threats. Nevertheless, sheriff's deputies screened everyone going into the Los Angeles Superior courtroom of Judge Sally Disco, who later ruled that Madonna should trim her trees. She had lost. But she was going to win the big one, the film role she believed was going to make her the greatest popular star in the world.

Madonna likes to talk, but she is careful about doing so because she feels that when she does she reveals too much of her personality. She does. Over the years she has not been able to resist and, brought together, her words give a new insight into how the self-styled little girl from Michigan became a champion of the so-called slut-feminism and one of the world's most famous people.

From when I was very young, I just knew that being a girl and being charming in a feminine sort of way could get me a lot of things, and I milked it for everything I could. I think your parents give you false expectations of life. All of us grow up with completely misguided notions about life and they don't change until you get out into the world. It's like someone telling you what love or marriage is: you can't know until you're there and you have to learn the hard way.

When I was a child, I always thought that the world was mine, that it was a stomping ground for me, full of opportunities. I always had this attitude that I was going to go out into the world and do all the things I wanted to do. Sometimes I travel through people, but I think that's true of most ambitious people. If the people can't go with me – whether it's a physical or emotional move – I feel sad about that. But that's part of the tragedy of love.

Every time I reach a new peak, I see a new one I want to climb. It's like I can't stop. Maybe I should rest and admire the view, but I can't. I've got to keep on pushing. Why? I don't know. I don't know what motivates me. I just know I've got to do it. You have to be patient. I'm not. The more money you have, the more problems you have. I went from making no money to making comparatively a lot and all I've had is problems. Life was simpler when I had no money, when I just barely survived.

There have been times when I've thought, 'If I'd known it was going to be like this, I wouldn't have tried so hard.' If it ever gets too much, or I feel like I'm being over-scrutinized, or I'm not enjoying it any more, then I won't do it. America is really a 'life-negative' society. People want to know all the underneath stuff, your dirty laundry, which isn't to say all the stuff the press has been getting on me is negative or dirty or whatever, but there's always a hope, for them, that they'll uncover something really scandalous.

You can't sit around worrying about people disliking you because they're always going to be there. It can't stop you. I could never have imagined that success could be like *this*, which was a surprise but I can handle it. I can still laugh about it, so I guess I'm alright. I think the ultimate challenge is to have some kind of style and grace even though you haven't got money, or standing in society, or formal education. I had a very middle-, lower-middle-class sort of upbringing, but I identify with people who have had, at some point in their lives, to struggle to survive. It adds another colour to your character.

I don't like violence. I never condoned hitting anyone, and I never thought that any violence should have taken place. I have chances to vent my anger in other ways other than confrontation. I like to fight people and kind of manipulate them into feeling like they're not being fought. I'd rather do it that way.

Music is still very important to me, but I always had a great interest in films, and the thought that I could only make records for the rest of my life filled me with horror. Ultimately I want to direct films.

They thought they would wake up one day and I'd go away. But I'm not going to go away. It's more than ego. It's an overwhelming interior light that I let shine without control. I am guided by my instinct . . . it's both my faith and conscience. I hate polite conversation. I hate it when people stand around and go, 'Hi, how are you?' I hate words that don't have any reason or meaning. Also I hate it when people smoke in elevators and closed-in places. It's just so rude. I have to listen to the criticism that I get when it's dealing with my work. It's beneficial, I guess, I don't take criticism very well but it's getting better. If I do something and there's 100 people in the room and 99 people say they liked it, I only remember the person who didn't like it.

I laugh at myself. I don't take myself completely seriously. I think that's another quality that people have to hold on to . . . you have to laugh, especially at yourself. I do it in most of the things I do, and most of the videos that I make and most of my performances. Even in my concerts there were so many moments when I just stood still and laughed at myself. I am ambitious. But if I weren't as talented as I am ambitious, I would be a gross monstrosity. I am not surprised by my success because it feels natural. I'm very indecisive: yes-no-yes. In my career, I make pretty good decisions, but in my personal life I cause constant havoc by changing my mind every five minutes.

My image is a natural extension of my performance, so my songs may not be deliberately sexual, but the way I achieve them could be. Women with blonde hair are perceived as much more sexual and much more impulsive . . . fun-loving but not as layered, not as deep, not serious . . . the artifice of being blonde has some incredible sort of sexual connotation. Men really respond to it. I like to leave the impression that Marilyn Monroe did, to be able to arouse so many different feelings in people. I always acted like a star long before I was one. If people don't see my sense of humour than I come off as being expensive, but I always endear myself to people when I find their weaknesses and they acknowledge it. It's the people who try to hide everything and try to make you think they're so cool that I can't stand. I think if someone becomes hugely successful, the public becomes disgusted with them and begins to wish the star would slip on a banana peel. That's the basic aspect of human nature.

I think women are intimidated by women who are incredibly ambitious or competitive because it's easier to deal with girls who aren't. It's easier to deal with people who aren't. But I never really think consciously of the fact that I'm a girl or anything like that. In fact, I think I've had advantages because I'm a girl. People have this idea that if you're sexual and beautiful and provocative, then there's nothing else you could possibly offer. People have always had that image about women. And while it might have seemed like I was behaving in a stereotypical way, at the same time, I was also masterminding it. I was in control of everything I was doing, and I think when people realized that, it confused them. People say I've set back the women's movement thirty years – but I think that women weren't ashamed of their bodies in the fifties. They luxuriated in their femininity and believed whole-heartedly in it. Women aren't like men. They can do things that men can't, mentally and physically. If people don't get the humour in my act, then they don't want to get it.

The good life is to just stay in music, where I've already established myself and it's easier. I will continue to write music as long as I'm inspired. I'm inspired; I feel inspired. Just to believe in the goodness of life and to believe in yourself. That may sound silly, but that's what it really comes down to, because you can get pretty cynical about life . . . it's nice to be able to sit back and think that there is innate goodness in people in the world despite all the crazy bulls . . . that you see presented in front of you every time you read the newspapers.

I have this feeling that I'm a bad girl – and that I need to be punished. I am what I am, and I do what I do. I never set out to be a role model for girls or women – and I don't conform to any stereotype. You know the idea: you need to be a chainsaw or an army tank to play in a man's world. Well, I don't act like a man, yet I play in a man's world. Irony is my favourite thing. Everything I do is meant to have several meanings, to be ambiguous. I knew I was up against a lot. I'm from a world they have no respect for. It was a really good experience for me to prove myself in that context.

There was a point in my life when I wanted to be a Peggy Guggenheim – be this patron of artists, have a gallery and a great art collection. When I'm really, really old, that's what I want to do. She had a wild life. I like that. I've basically gone wildly out of control. My manager gets insane about what I spend. But it placates me to put my energy into that work. I could be buying a Ferrari, but I'd rather spend it this way. I think the public is tired of trying to figure out whether I'm a feminist or not. I don't think of what I'm doing as gender specific. I am what I am, and I do what I do.

There is a wink behind everything I do. The public shouldn't think about this. Part of the reason I'm successful is because I'm a good businesswoman, but I don't think it is necessary for people to know that. All that means is that I'm in charge of everything that comes out. God! People say no to me all the time, but I guess the balance is tipped in the yes direction. If they do say no, you can be sure there will be a tantrum to follow.

I admit I have this feeling that I'm a bad girl and I need to be punished. The part of me that goes around saying 'Fuck you! Fuck you! I'm throwing this in your face!' is the part that's covering up the part that's saying 'I'm hurt. And I've been abandoned and I will never need anyone again.' So, here – have a stereotype! I don't make fun of Catholicism. I deeply respect Catholicism – its mystery and fear and oppressiveness, its passion and its discipline and its obsession with guilt. I hate waste and I hate to waste money. I don't see the point of having more than one car. And I hate to waste food.

Nothing that happened to me was a bad thing. Maybe I've had moments of frustration or felt that I was being misjudged or felt that I had painted myself into a corner. But in the end, everything that happened to me was good. I get letters from guys in jail all the time, too, but they just want to have a date with me. Most people that don't like me are people that are fanatically religious. No one can ever just play themselves in a movie. That's ridiculous. Obviously there can be a lot of things in the character that are like you, but you've got to be a little bit inventive or imaginative. I mean, there are certain things in the character that I can relate to, but I'm not playing myself, for God's sake!

It would also be nice to play some unsympathetic characters. God knows, I have my bad side. Yeah, but I've never been offered one [villain]. I'm sort of naturally a pain in the ass. I naturally like to do things that rub people up the wrong way. No, that's wrong. Let me rephrase that. I just like being controversial. I guess. Even that doesn't sound right. But somehow it happens that way. It's more like 'Hey, well, you know how they always say things are this way? Well, they're not! Or they don't have to be.'

I believe that someone is protecting me. Otherwise I'd be dead. Otherwise that guy tonight would have gotten out of his car and beaten the shit out of me. Believe me. It would have happened if I weren't protected, because I can't resist mouthing off to people when they curse at me. One time a guy did that to me and I said, 'Fuck you, motherfucker.' I wasn't in my car; I was standing on the curb giving directions to my girlfriend. And this guy got out of his car. It was in the Valley. It always happens in the Valley. This big guy got out of his car and walked over to me and I was thinking, 'Oh, my God, he's going to beat the shit out of me.' I was cowering. And I turned into a person I've never been in my life. I said, 'I am sorry! I am truly sorry!' So I think someone is protecting me. I don't know if it's an angel. It could be the Devil. He could have his own hidden agenda.

I think most sensitive people have psychic power. I think a lot of innate psychic power has to do with just being really observant. My psychic powers show up in dreams. Or in knowing when people are going to call, or what people are going to say, or what they are going to do next. I just had dreams about being murdered all the time. The only remotely entertainment-oriented dream I ever had was one where I dreamed I kissed Robert Redford. I was in the sixth grade. And it has not come true. It was weird. I don't think I ever really had any fixation on him. But the dream was so vivid. I was really turned on. You know how you have a body spot that's sensitive or powerful? There's one for each sign. Mine is my back. I have a great back. It's beautiful, I can say that. I am not a scholar. I'm a sponge. I just soak things up.

Maybe because everyone shits on me so much they felt sorry for me. I get a lot of bad press. I get ripped to shreds. I've got everybody waiting to tear me down. I'm good-for-nothing, no-talent has-been, and they can't wait until I drop dead.

Do I know what to do with my money? Yes, I do. Buy art, and invest money in writing good scripts, and give it to people who need it. Having money is just the best thing in the world. It gives you freedom and power and the ability to help other people. I know what to do with my money.

Since I was seventeen and moved to New York, I haven't needed his [her father's] help. We're the closest when I'm in a very vulnerable state. The great thing is that when I am, he's there for me. The rest of the time I roam around the world like a miniature tank. The end of the 'Oh Father' video, where I'm dancing on my mother's grave, is an attempt to embrace and accept my mother's death. My mother had a lot of us in the same month. She kept getting pregnant at the same time every year.

I had my chart done once. I remember only two things from it. One was that I should eat more cooked vegetables. The other was that I was going to meet an older man who was going to be a great influence on me. And then I met Warren Beatty. I love candy, as you can see. I'm a sugar junkie. It's because I was deprived of love as a child. I'm just kidding. I wasn't deprived. But I wasn't allowed to eat candy. That's really the reason. I've been gorging ever since I moved out of the house.

You know how religion is. Guys get to do everything. They get to be altar boys. They get to stay out late. Take their shirts off in the summer. They get to pee standing up. They get to fuck a lot of girls and not worry about getting pregnant. Although that doesn't have anything to do with being religious. Well, I moved to New York and went after my dreams. It takes a lot of devotion and discipline, and I think the combination of that and my upbringing has helped me to be as productive as I am.

You know, I can think of isolated moments where I could have given in and it would have made things better. But, all in all, I'm not with any of the people I'm not with for a much larger reason; we just weren't meant to be. If I'd changed and given in – or what I conceived to be giving in – to certain concessions that people had asked of me, maybe the relationships would have been successful, on the one hand, but then I would have had to give up other things in my career. And then I would have been miserable. So it's hard to say.

I mean, I do look around and go, God, it's great I have fame and fortune, but then I see Mia Farrow on the set with her baby, and I think she seems absolutely content. She has a huge family and that just seems like the most important thing. And, you know, love and everything, I don't really have that, but time hasn't run out for me yet. I'm not exactly sure who I'm looking for. I wish I knew . . . I wonder if I could ever find someone like me . . . I would probably kill them if I did.

I love performing, but it is very taxing to go on the road and travel in a bus. Video has made it possible to reach the masses without touring. I don't think about the work I do in terms of feminism. I certainly feel that I give women strength and hope, particularly young women. So in that respect, I feel my behaviour is feminist. But I'm certainly not militant about it, nor do I exactly premeditate it. So I think sex is equated with power in a way, and that's scary. It's scary for men that women should have that power – or to have that power and be sexy at the same time. I like to have control over most of the things in my career but I'm not a tyrant. I don't have to have it on my album that it's written, arranged, produced, directed and stars Madonna. To me, to have total control means you can lose objectivity. What I like is to be surrounded by really talented, intelligent people you can trust. And ask them for their advice and get their input. But let's face it, I'm not going to make an album and not show up for the vocals or make a video and have nothing to do with the script.

Music is the main vector of celebrity. When it's a success its impact is just as strong as a bullet hitting the target. Most of my lyrical ideas come from everyday life. Some are more fantasy motivated along the lines of ideal relationships. In general, my songs are a bit of both. When you are singing a song you are making yourself very vulnerable. It's almost like crying in front of people. Acting is like that, too. It's just a different way of doing it. Everything inspires me: a great book or movie, an expression in someone's eyes, children or old men walking down the street. You know what I like to do when I go to parties? I like talking to the butler and the janitors and stuff – they're the funniest, they inspire me.

I think people have too many pretentious ideas about music . . . what's artistic and what has integrity and what doesn't. They think if it's simple and accessible, then it's commercial and a total compromise. And if it's masked in mystery, not completely understood and slightly unattractive, it has integrity and is artistic. I don't believe that. I'm sure that each record I've heard influenced me in some way, just like every person you ever meet influences you.

I do in a way feel it would have been great in the old days [of Hollywood]. The studio system really nurtured and cared for you in a way it doesn't now. On the other hand, your life was not your own. Now you have more individual freedom, but you don't have anyone looking after your career in the way they did then.

So many times, I drive around in my expensive car and just think, 'God, I'm just a girl from Michigan.' It all seems so strange. Because I could never imagine it when I lived there. Those are the times I feel like I'm just a girl from Michigan.

EIGHTEEN

HOORAY FOR HOLLYWOOD

'The real secret to Madonna's success?

She puts curses on people and things to get what

she wants.'

AN ANONYMOUS 'FRIEND' TO AN AMERICAN NEWSPAPER IN 1991

Madonna the control freak. She says the perfect time of day, the time when she is happiest, is when the maids have gone. The bed is made-up perfect. The glasses are clean, the dishes stacked away. Everything is in its place. There is holiness in orderliness for Madonna. She can not, however, put on the telephone-answering machine. She needs to answer the phone.

A personal assistant travels everywhere with her; Madonna, like Cher and other popular icons, is treated like a baby. They may be tough don't-fuck-with-me-gals, but do not ask them to boil an egg. When a hand is held long enough, when an ego is stroked so much it shines, the routine of normal life gets lost. And with it vanishes a certain humanity. Those who believe they can have anything they want make their own often dangerous deity.

Eva Peron did. She is someone, like Monroe, who has always fascinated Madonna. And Madonna has understood the incredible screen potential of *Evita* since the success of the stage show. She fought hard to win the role.

Eva Peron went from being a peasant brunette to an upswept platinum-blonde and the heroine of her *descamisados* – 'the shirtless ones' – of Buenos Aires. She, like Madonna's mother, died early from cancer. 'Evita' Peron was thirty-three when the disease finally killed her in 1952. In 1976, Andrew Lloyd-Webber and Tim Rice turned the lady of the Casa Rosada, the lavish Pink Palace in Buenos Aires, into the unlikely subject of a rock opera. First, there was the record album and 'Don't Cry For Me Argentina' became a European hit single. By 1978 Australian entrepreneur Robert Stigwood and director Hal Prince – who had produced Lloyd-Webber's and Rice's *Jesus Christ Superstar* – staged the show in London to sensational reviews. Elaine Page became an overnight star. As did Patti Lupone when *Evita* arrived on Broadway. It had been the most coveted – and demanding – role on Broadway since Barbra Streisand appeared as Fanny Brice in *Funny Girl*.

Oh, what a movie it would make! A dozen actresses have flirted with the title role since 1979. Stigwood hired Ken Russell to direct a film version in Spain for Paramount Studios. In *Enfant terrible* Russell decided Liza Minnelli should star and not Elaine Page. Minnelli flew to London to make a test recording. 'Calling it a disaster would be one of the great understatements,' says Bill Oakes of RSO Films. The tape was destroyed at Minnelli's insistence, but Russell continued to want her as *Evita*. RSO Films and Russell later parted company on the project in 1991.

Video director Keith MacMillan then suggested doing *Evita* by 'shooting in a surrealistic soundstage environment'. There would be *interesting* guest casting like Boy George playing the Pope. 'We entertained the idea for about ten minutes,' says Oakes who said MacMillan saw the film like The Who's rock opera *Tommy*.

In the meantime a completely separate project was going on

and Ronald Harwood wrote a screenplay which director Marvin Chomsky, a master of the television mini-series format, turned into the 1981 film *Evita Peron*. The title role was taken by Faye Dunaway. Pebbles make more waves than it did.

In 1982, *Evita* went from Paramount Studios to Twentieth Century-Fox which was then headed by Sherry Lansing, the first female to attain such a position in Hollywood. She and director Herbert Ross saw the film as 'a swirling decadent fandango' and the star would be . . . Streisand or Ann-Margaret. Herbert Ross then left the project (he wanted too much money) and Streisand was not really interested. She knew she was too old for the role. It was Jon Peters, the former hairdresser and now Hollywood superpower, who was then her boyfriend, who had wanted Streisand to play the power-mad prima donna. Stigwood was interested in Meryl Streep but found 'unacceptable' the condition that Mike Nichols (*The Graduate, Working Girl*) be the director. Directors like Alan Pakula, Francis Coppola and Luis Puenzo were talked to and about.

Then the Weintraub Entertainment Group (WEG), headed by superbly connected Jerry Weintraub, struck a deal over financing and distribution of the film. Oliver Stone was to direct, and in the summer of 1988 scouted locations in Argentina. She went to the birthplace of Maria Eva Duarte: 'It was a lonely spot on the immense pampas where she grew up and I talked to people that still remember her. I wanted to do a film which would be beyond all political resentments and demagogic speculation.'

Stone said he was considering several actresses to play 'Evita'. They were an eclectic bunch: Streisand, the Australian singer and *Grease* actress Olivia Newton-John, and Madonna. Stone would not say if he was considering Patti Lupone.

Madonna had meetings. And meetings. She and Stone are both big egos and there were plenty seismic tremblers from the talks as their egos snagged like the subterranean plates grinding on an earthquake fault line. Stigwood wanted Hector Babenco, the director who won an Oscar nomination for *Kiss of the Spider Woman,* to guide the production. And he wanted Madonna as the star. Babenco was frustrated by the negotiations and moved on to other projects.

Stone did not like that. And that thinking had lined Madonna and Babenco. That did not sit well with Stone who was now into the mainstream with projects like *Platoon* and *Wall Street* and was about to start work on *Born on the Fourth of July*. Christ, he was making a movie starring Tom Cruise, the biggest star in Hollywood at that moment. Madonna? Hell, who needed the aggravation?

'We decided on certain things before production,' says Bill Oakes, explaining:

We wouldn't dub the voice. It had to be somebody who could act and sing. Madonna asked us if she could be considered and she remained under consideration until she and Stone fell out. It would have been difficult to conceive of them working together.

Madonna felt she was kept away from the facts: was it going to be an operetta? A straight drama? A musical with dialogue? She felt she had made enough mistakes in movies. But, although she and Stone disagreed, she was determined that one day ... Madonna went on the record saying: 'I've decided that if anybody is going to do it, I'm going to do it.'

Stone and Meryl Streep met in the summer of 1989 and in August the Oscar-winning actress, who is also a classically trained singer, sang much of the *Evita* score. Streep, like Madonna, a hard-working perfectionist, was taking twice-weekly diva and tango lessons with singer-choreographer Paula Abdul. Stone had completed the script which was described as 'a politically charged love story'. The original score was intact apart from one song. In Hollywood parlance 'the package' of Stone and Streep was complete.

Streep's tape was sent to London. Lloyd-Webber and Tim Rice were not totally convinced. An RSO source said the praise was not lavish but along the lines of 'she can carry a tune'.

Jerry Weintraub's company was having its own problems after a string of Hollywood flops like Kim Basinger's *My Stepmother is an Alien*. Oliver Stone moved on to his Jim Morrison biopic, *The*

Doors. Streep, ungraciously, also went through the revolving *Evita* door. She was disgruntled at 'wasting' a year on the project.

And after Madonna got what she wanted – the title role of *Evita* – Streep sniped: 'I can sing better than she can if that counts for anything.'

Madonna had won by maintaining her stance. While others argued, she kept advertising her interest at meetings with the men that matter – the moneymen known as 'the suits'. They sit in tower blocks and decide how to spend millions of dollars. A wrong decision and they have to find another game to play.

Madonna as *Evita*. Certainly bankable and certainly worth a gamble. Especially for Jeffrey Katzenberg, the great Madonna fan at the Disney Studios. Since *Dick Tracy*, he and Madonna had maintained contact. Officially, the studio called it 'a continuing creative agreement'.

Stigwood, Lloyd-Webber and Co. were now involved with Glen Gordon Carron the creator, and often writer, of the success-ful Cybill Shepherd–Bruce Willis television series *Moonlighting*. Carron would direct the film from his own screenplay which by spring 1991 was being called 'great'.

Disney, keen to keep the budget under $30 million, were having more meetings. But the project was 'hot'. Cingeri Pro-ductions, led by Andy Vajna, who made a fortune with the *Rambo* films, wanted some of the action. Cingeri's films are distributed in America by Disney, but early in the talks it was clear Katzenberg was carefully monitoring Disney's interest in *Evita*. And so was Madonna. Britain's Jeremy Irons, an Oscar winner for his wicked portrayal of Claus Von Bulow in *Reversal of Fortune*, was the actor wanted for Juan Peron. When Glenn Gordon Carron met with Irons, his title star was also present. Not only had Madonna won her role, she had negotiated conditions which gave her a say, some control over the final film. Her time with Warren Beatty had not been wasted.

Madonna was also happy publicly to display her enthusiasm. She agreed to present Andrew Lloyd-Webber with an award saluting his work at the Los Angeles Music Centre Benefactors' dinner at the Beverly Wilshire Hotel. A politically correct crowd as well as celebrities attended. Madonna arrived fifteen minutes late wearing a black sheath of a dress and platinum hair and a crowd of bodyguards snapping 'Get Back' at preying pararazzi. On stage, she livened up the mainly staid audience by calling up Lloyd-Webber with: 'Andrew? Where are you, you bad boy?' Lloyd-Webber is bemused by his *Evita* star: 'I think I'm going to have an interesting and remarkable collaboration. My goodness, she's a good girl.'

Goodness, as we know, had nothing to do with it. It was hard-headed business. And Madonna was not putting all her film hopes in one production basket. She had not wasted her time waiting to get the *Evita* title role. While the negotiations were going on, she was playing an acrobat in an, as usual, untitled Woody Allen film. It sounded as though they were getting on well. He called her 'prima donna' and she called him 'little twerp'.

There were other film projects. In the autumn of 1991 she began work on *A League of Their Own*, a film described by the producers as 'about a worldly ballplayer with a sharp tongue and a fast reputation'. The project first involved Debra Winger but then Madonna took the role of Mae in the story about a female baseball team in the 1940s. The director is Penny Marshall and Madonna's co-star is Tom Hanks, who starred in Marshall's enormously successful film *Big*.

Madonna decided to make *A League of Their Own* while waiting for a starting date for *Evita*. The Disney Studios chairman, Jeffrey Katzenberg, had made a vow of film budget austerity and the $30 million price tag for *Evita* seemed too much for him. But the Lloyd-Webber/Robert Stigwood/Glen Gordon Carron/Madonna package remains intact and Paramount Studios is now the likely winner in the race to make the film.

Madonna continues to cast her net around other movies. Freddy DeMann confirmed that Madonna wanted to star as the late Martha Graham, the mother of modern American dance. She also has the rights to *Little Odessa* about a Russian girl in Brooklyn. And she and Demi Moore from *Ghost* were going to be

Leda and Swan in an action film along the lines of *Lethal Weapon*. Madonna and Moore spent the early part of 1991 working on the script. Producer Joel Silver, who made the *Die Hard* movies with Moore's husband Bruce Willis and also the two big hit *Lethal Weapons* with Mel Gibson and Danny Glover, planned two *Leda and Swan* film sequels before the first was even filmed. Madonna as Mel Gibson? If you follow the formula, she must eventually play Lady Macbeth.

And she probably will. She is determined to be a major box-office movie star, a screen idol. It is in her voice. Listen:

I've been a failure so far. And the reason is that I simply haven't put a lot of thought into it. I haven't honoured or respected a movie career the way I should have. I didn't approach it the way I approached by music career. I'd had a lot of success in music, and all of a sudden people are going, '*Here's a movie.*' And I didn't think about it. I just took it. I underestimated the power of the medium. It's been a good lesson for me.

Dick Tracy?

You could say I have a lot of unresolved feelings about it. I remember being very upset that all of my big music scenes were cut up the way they were. I learned a lot about film-making from Warren, but obviously it didn't make me a big box-office star, did it?

She will do everything to make sure *Evita* does, including what amounts to corporate creeping.

'There's a lot of business stuff,' says Madonna about the long negotiations she says she turns into a little voyeuristic fun for businessmen:

I live for meeting with the Suits. I love them because I know they had a really boring week and I walk in there with my orange-velvet leggings and drop popcorn in my cleavage and then fish it out and eat it. I like that. I know I'm entertaining them and I know that they know. The best meetings are with Suits who are intelligent because then things are operating on a whole other level.

The Suits see Madonna as a female Stallone/Schwarzenegger of the nineties.

At the Oscars, she looked like Marilyn Monroe.

She and Michael Jackson were the oddball sensation. He had

worn collagen-pumped lips while signing his billion-dollar contract with Sony Records. She wears the Hollywood full-lipped
look in her controversial 1991 *Truth or Dare: On the Road, Behind the
Scenes, and In Bed with Madonna* documentary. Madonna has something to sell at the Oscars as well as herself.

Jackson wore two gloves, gold-tipped cowboy boots and a
dazzling diamond brooch at his throat, his hair hanging down his
back and around his often sculpted face. Madonna was a peroxide
picture in a felony low-cut pearl-encrusted Bob Mackie shimmer-
ing white gown. The $20 million in diamonds – borrowed for the
evening from legendary New York jeweller Harry Winston –
included a 34-carat pink diamond valued at $14 million, which
was reset for the evening into Madonna's ring size. The baubles
added extra twinkle to what headline writers were the next day
calling the date of the century. Imagine if it was a *real* date –
the genetic possibilities of little Madonna and Michaels?
Twinkle, twinkle little stars. But who would grab which crotch?
No. No.

It was business. Madonna and Jackson took the two front-row
seats in the aisle, centre stage at the Shrine Auditorium. Madonna
was perfectly positioned as Jeremy Irons was named Best Actor
for *Reversal of Fortune*. As Irons made his way to the stage, she
leaped up with a congratulatory hug and kiss eager for the
celebrity audience to see how close she and the man she-wanted-
to-be-Juan were. A billion people watch the Academy Awards on
television: this was heavyweight public relations.

As Madonna worked this world-wide 'room' Michael Jackson
gazed merrily into space.

There was little space a few hours later at Spago, the now
obligatory Oscar-night hangout. Wolfgang Puck's restaurant is a
star spot all year, but on Oscar night agent Irving 'Swifty' Lazar
takes it over and it is invitation only. In 1991, Donald Trump
could not even buy entry. Madonna and Michael waltzed in to the
A-table watched by Israeli security guards. They sat with
Anjelica Huston and Michael and Diandra Douglas. Al Pacino
nodded to Madonna who showed him some cleavage. Jack Lem-

mon stared. Jeremy Irons found *Reversal* co-star Glenn Close for a chat. Jodie Foster arrived in a breast-bearing Armani jacket.

Actors. Popular and honoured ones. Madonna liked the company. Warren Beatty – his *Dick Tracy* took three Oscars – sat with French director Louis Malle and his wife Candice Bergen. Beatty's new lover, model Stephanie Seymour, was not with him. In a moment, Madonna was over and sniggering with Beatty and then sitting in his lap as he fondly fondled her. Madonna squealed: 'It's so unbelievable. What a night!' She sounded like a girl from the Midwest. Steve Bray, the loyal, longest serving soldier on the Madonna racing team smiled: 'She was always like this. She wanted attention – now it's her job.'

Truth or Dare got attention (the London premiere, with the more provocative title *In Bed With Madonna*, was shown to packed audiences in July 1991). This was a home movie like *sex, lies and videotape* is to *Bambi*. The beautiful Alek Keshishian – handsome is redundant for the long-haired, brown-eyed man – directed the film. Madonna allowed him, his cameras and microphones access to almost all her waking moments, but she did not fall for his charms: 'I found Alek quite attractive, but I kept my distance because I never like to have a crush on somebody everybody else has a crush on.'

It didn't inhibit. She demonstrated her artfulness at oral sex by showing her gulping style on a plastic bottle of Evian water. She sang a song about farting. She ogles as two men kiss and shouts: 'Oh God! I'm getting a hard-on.' Later, she would reveal: 'That's my favourite scene in the movie. I love that people are going to watch that and go home and talk about it all night long. I live for things like that.'

There are other things to talk about. For the first time since her father's remarriage, she visited her mother's grave. In the film, she lies on top of her mother's grave and wonders if her mother is 'just a bunch of dust'. In an unedited three-hour black and white tape, she frolicks with one of her male dancers on the Blonde

Ambition Tour and he rips off his clothes as she shouts at him: 'Your cock is big.' In another sequence another clearly wanting dancer is reprimanded: 'Get out of my bed and don't come back until your cock is bigger.'

She calls Warren Beatty 'a pussy man'. She appears topless. Kevin Costner appears backstage after her Blonde Ambition appearance in Los Angeles and tells her: 'You were great. We thought it was neat.' After he goes, Madonna puts her finger down her throat and says: 'Anybody who says my show is neat *has* to go.' Bootleg copies of the unedited documentary were selling in Hollywood for between $8,000 and $30,000 depending on film quality.

Warren Beatty wanted some scenes of him deleted before the film went into the world's cinemas. He does nothing naughty on film – he just did not want to be associated with it. But Madonna's graveyard 'meeting' with her mother and most of the other incidents remained when the film was released in the High Street cinemas. One of the Beatty scenes that remained was one of the most intimate. Madonna is being examined by a throat specialist at her New York apartment. As the doctor is at work, Beatty is off camera and muttering about the insanity of filming the medical exam. When the doctor turns and asks if Madonna wants to talk off-camera, Beatty loses his cool: 'She doesn't want to *live* off-camera! What point is there to existing?'

Beatty made a point of avoiding the Hollywood première of Madonna's indulgent *Truth or Dare* in May 1991. He clearly did not want to be in a situation where he might be asked to comment on the film. The special-invitation-only screening at the Cineramadome was to benefit the AIDS Project Los Angeles and the AIDS Action Foundation. The post-screening party was held at the Arena night-club, one of Los Angeles' most popular gay clubs. It was quite an evening.

Madonna appeared and at first was not recognized. Gone was the Marilyn-look. In its place was something close to Morticia from the sixties' black-and-white cult television series, and a British favourite of the time, *The Addams Family*, which in 1991 was revamped as a big-budget feature film starring Anjelica Huston as Morticia and Raul Julia as her husband. Madonna wore long, brown hair, a Jean-Paul Gaultier catsuit and black eyeliner almost to her ears. The snake had slipped another skin. Marilyn one moment, Morticia the next.

Things were more familiar at the Arena where many of the 700 invited guests gathered later. Her brother Christopher was there and David Geffen and actress Mimi Rogers, the former Mrs Tom Cruise, Barry Manilow, Steven Seagal, Matthew Modine, Rosanna Arquette, super-producer Joel Silver, Vanilla Ice and a host of enormous drag queens. So was Sandra Bernhard. Madonna was mostly a good girl. Bernhard was her outrageous, suggestive, uninhibited self. The two girls rubbed up against each other suggestively to the delight of the Arena audience.

Truth or dare?

At the 1991 Cannes Film Festival, Madonna hosted a small dinner party where the guests played truth or dare, the game that gave her film its title. Designer Jean-Paul Gaultier dared Madonna to French kiss actress Anne Parillaud, the star of *La Femme Nikita*. She did.

Madonna was having fun publicly playing her game. But what was even more revealing in 1991 than the film *Truth or Dare* was an interview Madonna gave to the New-York-based gay magazine, *Advocate*. It quickly became known as the most faxed article in Hollywood.

Mainstream Hollywood was amazed at what Madonna had to say. She is asked: 'How big is Warren Beatty's dick?' And the shock was not her answer, but that she even acknowledged the question. As she did questions about whether Beatty may have gay leanings. But the big question: The Beatty dick? Her answer: 'I haven't measured it, but it's a perfectly wonderful size.'

She admitted her 'agency' was 'freaking' about her being demeaning on the film about Kevin Costner and she adds:

'Cause Kevin Costner is like this big hero and everything. But, I mean, come on; people rip me to shreds every chance they get and I can take it so he should be able to take it.

Emasculating? Now, look you can only take the balls away from people when they give them to you. I enjoy expressing myself and if I think someone is being a pussy I say it.

She was asked if she was personally kinky.

What do you mean by kinky? I am aroused by two men kissing. Is that kinky? I am aroused by the idea of a woman making love with me while either a man or another woman watches. Is that kinky?

She says she has not used dildos or sex toys: 'I like the human body. I like flesh. I like things that are living and breathing. And a finger will do just fine. I've never owned a vibrator.'

In the *Advocate* interview Madonna sets herself up as a feminist heroine. A social politician? No taboo was too much for discussion.

Whether it is regarded as shameless or heroic it got the world talking about issues – and Madonna. She got jumped on and dumped on for her film and for her interview, but emerged as still the world's most interesting pop icon. And most stimulating.

But by 1991 Tony Ward, who had become her lover during and after co-starring in the 'Justify My Love' video, was out of her life. It seems she can always – as the Oscar song goes – get her man. Keeping him is the problem.

EPILOGUE

ALONE ON
THE HILL

'I long for children.'

MADONNA IN 1991

Tony Ward, because of his Madonna association, became the focus of much newspaper interest and it was discovered that after he and Madonna had become intimate, he married another woman. But the marriage certificate showing Ward and Amalia Papadimos, twenty-three, a Greek citizen, in Las Vegas, was not welcome to Madonna. She had *Evita*. She hadn't got her man.

I wish I were married and in a situation where having a child would be possible. People say: 'Well, have one on your own.' I say: 'Wait a minute, I'm not interested in raising a cripple.' I want a father there. I want someone I can depend on.

And, like Garbo, how long before she wants to be alone?

Madonna believes in fate. A fortune teller told her in 1991 that her heart would be broken, that she would not have children.

That upset her. Then, the fortune teller told her that she was not suited to her career choices. That devastated her. Madonna got drunk. For the first time in her life she lost control.

A story published in America said she had bought a crypt so she could be buried near Marilyn Monroe at Westwood Memorial Park. She hasn't. Yet.

INDEX

AIDS
  Charities 136, 190
  test for 50
Academy Awards *see* Oscars
Adjani, Isabelle 144
Advocate magazine 191–2
Aiello, Danny 92
Albergate, Al 124
Allen, Woody 186
Allred, Gloria 92
Alvin Ailey American Dance
  Theatre 40
America's Planned
  Parenthood 91
Arquette, Rosanna 60–61, 191
At Close Range 72–4

Babenco, Hector 183–4
Barbone, Camille 37, 46, 47–8
Barrymore, Drew 93
Barrymore, John 70
Beastie Boys 61
Beatty, Warren 190, 191
  and *Dick Tracy* 121–2, 143–5
  background 145–7
  relationship with Madonna
    136–7, 139–42, 145, 149–52,
    165, 168
Belanger, Carol 20, 22, 28, 73
Benitez, John 'Jellybean' 52, 54,
  57, 61–2, 165
Bergen, Candice 189
Bernhard, Sandra 116–20, 121,
  153, 154, 191
  lesbian relationships, talk
    of 117, 120
Blonde Ambition Tour 159–60,
  162–4
Bloodhounds of Broadway 116
Bonazza, Cesare 97

Borrahlho, Leonel 86–7
Bowie, David 89
Branca, John 171
Brat Pack 63, 65, 69
Bray, Steve 35–6, 47–8, 49,
  51–2, 189
  song-writing 54, 90–91
Breakfast Club band 41, 45
Bridges, Beau 151
Bridges, Jeff 151
Broderick, Matthew 116
Brookner, Howard 136
  death from AIDS 116
Burgoyne, Martin 51
  death from AIDS 104, 116

Cannon, Dyan 118
Canonero, Milena 154
Caron, Leslie 144, 146
Carron, Glen Gordon 185, 186
Carson, Johnny 79
  Chat Show 103
Cates, Phoebe 63
Cazalet, Amanda 170
Certain Sacrifice, A 39, 84
Chaplin, Peter 160–61
Chapman, John 55
Cher 80, 107
Chomsky, Marvin 183
Christie, Julie 144
Ciccone, Anthony (brother) 9
Ciccone, Christopher (brother)
  11, 19, 129, 135, 153, 171, 191
Ciccone, Gaetano (grandfather)
  5–8
Ciccone, Jennifer (half-sister) 18
Ciccone, Joan (née Stone)
  (stepmother) 18
Ciccone, Madonna (née Fortin)
  (mother) 9–13

death from cancer 11–13
Ciccone, Madonna Louise
    Veronica see Madonna
Ciccone, Mario (half-brother)
    18, 112, 169
Ciccone, Martin (brother) 9, 19
Ciccone, Melanie (sister) 11
Ciccone, Melissa (sister) 24
Ciccone, Michelina
    (grandmother) 5–8
Ciccone, Paula (sister) 10, 14,
    22, 70, 80
Ciccone, Silvio 'Tony' (father)
    8–11, 13–15, 20–22, 40, 53, 61,
    79
Clark, Dick 130
Close, Glenn 117, 189
Coati Mundi 104
Collins, Joan 142, 144
Colors 97–9
Costner, Kevin 190, 191
Cottrell, Laurence 74, 83
Crystal, Billy 3
Currie, Alannah 77

Daly, John 81
Daulton, Andrew Lee 66
DeMann, Freddy (manager) 54,
    69, 84–5, 131–2, 136, 168,
    186
DeNiro, Robert 66
Desperately Seeking Susan 60–61,
    68
Dick Tracy 121, 136–7, 139–45,
    150–52, 154, 165
Dillon, Matt 116
DiMaggio, Joe 63
Disco, Judge Sally 171
Douglas, Diandra 188
Douglas, Michael 188
Dunaway, Faye 140, 183
Dunne, Griffin 96
Duvall, Robert 93, 97, 99
Dylan, Bob 89

Easton, Sheena 107
Eastwood, Clint 81
Elliot, Brian 91–2
Estevez, Emilio 65, 68
Evita 84, 88, 120–21, 130, 182–7

Falcon and the Snowman, The 66
Farrell, Robert 170
Fawcett, Farrah 93
First Parents Resources Centre
    92
Flynn, Christopher 30–33, 135
    death from AIDS 33
Foley, James 72, 73, 80, 96, 109
Fonda, Jane 146
Fortin, Michael (uncle) 9
Foster, Jodie 189
Frederick's of Hollywood 55
Frey, Olen 93
Friedlander, Lee 38–9

Gair, Joanne 164
Gaultier, Jean-Paul 161, 163,
    164, 191
Geffen, David 136, 155, 191
Gibson, Debbie 134
Gilbert, Jonathon 30
Gilroy, Dan 40, 41, 45–6
Gilroy, Ed 40, 45–6
Gore, Tipper 92
Gorrard, Jim 88
Grant, Lee 146
Grey, Jennifer 116, 153
Guilio, Bambina de 106

Hall, Peter 146
Hanks, Tom 186
Harris, Jayme 169
Harrison, George 85, 87–90
Hart, Gary 122
Harwood, Ronald 183
Hauer, Rutger 116
Heckerling, Amy 64
Helena 108
Hemingway, Mariel 76–7
Henry, Buck 141

Hernandez, Patrick 41, 43–4
High Society magazine 39
Hilburn, Robert 91
Hoffman, Dustin 2, 141
Hopper, Dennis 97–9
Huang, Nancy 76
Huston, Anjelica 93, 188, 190
Hutton, Tim 63, 66

Idol, Billy 73, 108
Immaculate Collection, The album 169
In Bed With Madonna see *Truth or Dare*
Irons, Jeremy 185, 188, 189

Jackson, LaToya 134–5
Jackson, Michael 2, 54, 158, 163, 187–8
Jagger, Mick 69
Jahns, Lori 11, 22
Janus, Sam 55
Johnson, Don 73, 91
Judgement in Berlin 101–2
'Justify My Love' video 169–70

Kahlo, Frida 128–9, 153–4
Kamins, Mark 48, 49–52
Kartvedt, Sindre 113
Katzenberg, Jeffrey 130, 137, 143, 185, 186
Keaton, Diane 73–4, 141
Kennedy, John F, Jr 73
Keshishian, Alek 189
Kindness of Women 105
Klein, Jeffrie 98–9
Knight, Philip 134
Krall, Libby 89

Lang, Pearl 40
Lansing, Sherry 64, 183
Law, Lindsay 116
Lazar, Irving 'Swifty' 188
League of Their Own, A 186
Lemmon, Jack 188–9
Leonard, Patrick 90–91, 130

Letterman, David 120, 153
Lewicki, Stephen 39
Lewis, Jerry 118
Like a Prayer album 131, 134
Like a Virgin album 53, 54, 56, 61
  Tour 71–3
Live Aid 75
Lloyd-Webber, Andrew 121, 130, 182, 184, 185–6
Long, Russell 28, 73
Lucas, Reggie 49, 52–3
Lupone, Patti 182, 183

MTV 71, 133
  bans *Justify My Love* 170
McGovern, Elizabeth 64–5
Mackenzie, Todd 131–2
MacLaine, Shirley 145, 165
MacMillan, Keith 182
McSweeney, Lieut Bill 122–4
Madonna (Madonna Louise Veronica Ciccone)
  birth 10
  early childhood 10–15, 17–18
  mother's death from cancer 11–13, 14–15, 112
  dance classes 14, 30–33, 40
  father's remarriage 18
  schooldays 19–27
  church talent show 20–21
  friendships 20–27
  sexual experimentations 28, 29
  Marilyn Monroe, obsession with 25, 29–30, 62, 72, 182
  homosexuality, awareness of 32–3
  moves to New York 33, 35–7
  modelling work 37–9
  A Certain Sacrifice 39, 84
  Breakfast Club band 40–41, 45–6
  Paris trip 42–5
  sexual encounters 46, 50
  Madonna band 47–8, 50–51

Madonna (*cont*)
  BOY TOY label 46, 50, 56
  'Everybody' 51, 53
  'Burning Up' 51–2
  Madonna album 52–3
  videos 53, 54–5
  Like a Virgin album 53–6, 61,
    71–2
  Freddy DeMann as manager
    54
  'ban Madonna' outcries 55–6
  Desperately Seeking Susan 60, 68
  Like a Virgin Tour 61, 69
  meets Sean Penn 62
  visits Monroe's grave 63
  early relationship with Penn
    70, 72–4
  vegetarianism 71, 106, 159–61
  wedding 75–81
  honeymoon 81–2
  house-hunting 82
  psychiatric treatment 83, 136,
    167
  Evita, title role 84, 120, 182–7
  Shanghai Surprise 85–9
  Hong Kong, problems in 86–8
  London, unpopularity in
    89–90
  True Blue album 90–92
  'Papa Don't Preach', outcry
    over 91–2
  Penn's violence, reactions to
    95–7, 97–9
  Who's That Girl? 96–7
    Tour 101–5
  physical training 101–2,
    158–60
  meets Italian relatives 106
  pregnancy, hopes of 107
  divorce proceedings 108–9,
    125–6
  cancer, fear of 112–13
  Broadway debut 114–16
  lesbian relationships, talk of
    117, 119–20
  assaulted by Penn 122–4
  Hollywood home 127–9
  art collection 128–9
  Madonna Incorporated 128,
    130, 157
  Pepsi-Cola deal 131–3
  'Like a Prayer' video 131–3,
    134
  Niké endorsement 133–4
  earnings 135–7
  Warren Beatty, relationship
    with 137, 139–40, 142–4,
    149, 151, 165, 168
  Dick Tracy 139, 141–3, 150–52,
    154
  Madonna: I'm Breathless album
    144, 154
  costumes 154, 161–4
  Blonde Ambition Tour
    158–60, 162–4
  hairstyles 162
  Paris fashion shows 169
  Tony Ward, relationship with
    169, 192, 193
  'Justify My Love' video
    169–70
  reveals personality 172–9
  Truth or Dare 189–91
Madonna album 54
Madonna: I'm Breathless album
  144, 154
Madonna Incorporated 128,
  130, 157
Madonna Secrets Act 157
'Make a Wish' video 131–3
Malle, Louis 189
Mamet, David 114
Manilow, Barry 191
Mantegna, Joe 114–15
Maripol 50, 69
Marshall, Penny 186
Merrick, Judge John 79–80
Midler, Bette 75
Minnelli, Liza 182
Mitchell, Joni 118
Modine, Matthew 191
Mondino, Jean-Baptiste 170

Monroe, Marilyn, fascination
    with 25, 29–30, 62, 73, 182
  visit to grave 63
Montgomery, Meagan 99
Moore, Demi 186–7
Moran, Alfred 91
Moschino, Franco 161
Mosconi, Robert 133
Mosher, Gregory 115
Mugler, Thierry 169

National Organisation of
    Women 92
Natividad, Kitten 77
Nicholls, Robert 131
Nicholson, Jack 85, 141
Nightline TV show 171
Niké 133–4
Nixon, Chris 87–8

Oakes, Bill 182, 184
Ochs, Phil 81
O'Neal, Ryan 93, 95
Ono, Yoko 89
Orion Pictures 60, 68, 72
Oscar Ceremony 1–3, 158,
    187–8
  awards 154, 189
Ostin, Michael 81, 94–5

Pacino, Al 2, 141, 151–2, 188
Paige, Elaine 121, 182
Parillaud, Anne 191
Parr, Robert 158–9
Parsons, Estelle 141
Paterson, Vince 163
Pedall, Bert 136
Pellerin, Jean-Claude 43
Pellerin, Michelle 44
Penn, Christopher 63, 72
Penn, Leo 63, 65, 101
Penn, Sean
  meets Madonna 62
  background 63
  proposals 64–5
  Brat Pack 63, 65, 69

  early relationship with
    Madonna 70, 72–4
  violence, acts of 74, 83–4, 87,
    93–6, 97–9, 121
  wedding 75–81
  honeymoon 81–2
  prison 102–3, 105, 107
  divorce proceedings 108–9,
    125–6
  Casualties of War 114
  assault on Madonna 122–4
  Cannes Film Festival 168
Penthouse 39
Pepsi-Cola 131–3
Peters, Jon 183
Pfeiffer, Michelle 151
Phillips, Julia 84–5
Phillips, Michelle 144
Playboy 39
Pollard, Michael J 140, 141
Ponce, Dr Danilo 55
Prince, Hal 182

Quaid, Randy 116

Reagan, Nancy 82
Redgrave, Vanessa 115
Rice, Tim 121, 130, 182, 184
Ritts, Herb 129, 164, 169
Robinson, Donald 171
Rodgers, Nile 53, 54, 76
Rogers, Mimi 191
Roland, Lonny 152
Rosenberg, Liz 108
Rosenblatt, Michael 49–50
Rosenthal, Richard 64
Ross, Diana 54, 169, 189
Ross, Herbert 68–9, 183
Russell, Ken 182
Russell, Theresa 158
Ryan, Eileen (Mrs Leo Penn)
    63, 72, 78

Sanford, Midge 60
Santoni, Reni 64
Schindler, Paul 136

Schreiber, Martin 38–9
Scolinos, Henry 111
Scott, Margaret 56
Seagal, Stephen 191
Seidelman, Susan 59–60, 68
Seymour, Stephanie 189
Shanghai Surprise 85–90
Sheen, Charlie 68
Sheen, Martin 68, 88
Silver, Joel 187, 191
Silver, Ron 114–15
Simon, Neil 82
Sire Records 49–52
Smit, Angie 41, 45
Solo, Robert 98
Sondheim, Stephen 150, 154
Speed-the-Plow 114–15
Springsteen, Pam 64–5
Stanton, Harry Dean 64, 77, 93
Stark, Ray 69
Steel, Dawn 120
Stein, Seymour 51, 84
Steiner, Dr Jerrold 112–13
Stephens, Stephanie 120, 131
Stewart, Marlene 78, 115, 163
Stigwood, Robert 84, 182, 185–6
Stillbower, Steven 112
Stone, Bill 39
Stone, Oliver 120–21, 130, 151,
    183–4
Streep, Meryl 117, 183, 184–5
Streisand, Barbra 54, 76, 182,
    183
Sykes, John 71

Thompson Twins 75–7

Tolot, Francesca 162
Toms, Tony 159–60
Toy, Terence 81
Travilla, Bill 62
Trepanier, Mrs Sylvia 19
True Blue album 90–92
Trump, Donald 188
Truth or Dare 29, 189–91
Twomey, Rev Nick 25, 27–8

Unger, Kurt 79
United Parents Under God 56

Vajna, Andy 185
Van Lieu, Jean 43
Vidal, Victor 162
Vitucci, Amelia 106
Vitucci, Guiseppe 106

Wagner, Robert 146
Walken, Christopher 72, 80
Ward, Tony 169, 192, 193
Warden, Jack 140
Wehner, Deputy Sheriff Bill
    112
Weintraub, Jerry 183, 184
Weiss, Lauren 124
Weitzman, Howard 99
Who's That Girl? 96, 102
    Tour 101, 103–5
Wolinski, David 93–5
Wood, Natalie 144, 146

Young, Elaine 107

Zuffante, Vinnie 108